Bright Ideas
Games for PE

Contents

Published by Scholastic Publications Ltd,
Marlborough House, Holly Walk,
Leamington Spa, Warwickshire CV32 4LS.

© 1987 Scholastic Publications Ltd.

Reprinted 1987 1988 1989

Written by Pauline Wetton
Edited by Priscilla Chambers and
Jackie Cunningham-Craig
Illustrations by Jane Bottomley

Printed in Great Britain by
Loxley Brothers Ltd, Sheffield

ISBN 0 590 70690 X

Front and back cover: Martyn Chillmaid

Equipment for front cover supplied by C G Davies & Son (The Sports People) Ltd., Coventry

Artificial turf supplied by Balsam International Limited, Leicester.

Introduction

Games are part of our heritage and have, over the centuries, played a major part in our recreational lives. Today, there is still great interest in the major games as well as an encouraging upsurge of interest in what used to be classed as minority sports. Yet, children seem to be playing fewer playground games and in general, seem to be playing with friends after school to a much lesser degree than even ten years ago. This may be partly due to social conditions, but it could also be because games no longer hold the same significance in the primary school curriculum as they used to.

Games not only provide an excellent medium for developing particular skills. They also:

- Provide large and fine muscle development and control.
- Provide a vehicle for fitness and health development.
- Allow children to gain mental alertness.
- Development the children's understanding of some mathematical and scientific concepts.
- Increase the children's vocabulary and language concepts.
- Help them to understand the need to play fairly and the notion of good sportsmanship.
- Develop their social awareness and contribute to the children's moral development.

Successful games experience is dependent on the teacher playing a very important role in assessing children's needs both as individuals and as part of the class. Since games are not inherently fun, teachers have to guard against situations where a games lesson can become a negative or unhappy experience.

Class lessons which are of most value are those where children are active for most of the time. Sometimes activities have to be slightly restricted because of a lack of space or equipment, but if the general principle of 'most of the children active for most of the time' is adhered to then lessons will be much more productive.

Teaching style is very much a personal matter. In games, as in any other class activity, teachers know their own class better than anyone else.

Structure of book

To help teachers get started the lessons in this book are listed in sequential developmental order but obviously can be adjusted to correspond to the needs of particular children and their environments.

The ages given are intended as rough guidelines. The skills level of the children will depend upon what games experience they have had previously.

It is recommended that a general framework for each lesson should be adopted. This should consist of:

Warming up exercises. These have been chosen so as to either complement the lesson or provide a contrast.
Skill training. This is the learning time. Teachers should be teaching a new skill or letting the children practise and refine a known skill. Repetition is very important.
Games or activities. This part of the lesson should be used to practise the skills learned within a game context wherever possible.

A section on pre-athletic skills is included so that those schools which have a sports day can do practise running, throwing and jumping. It is important that if athletic skills are to be used, they are taught properly, and the correct terminology used.

Pre-sport skills are included to help those schools where netball, soccer, and rounders are introduced for older children. Teachers are urgently requested to follow the advice of the governing bodies of these sports and not try to teach children of this age to play a full sided game or to use a full size pitch, particularly in a class lesson. Activities should be based on small sided games with fewer and simpler rules to give more opportunities for individual development and involvement.

Five and ten minute fillers have also been included: these can be used whenever a teacher needs extra activities to lengthen a lesson or to give more practice at certain skills.

Planning the lesson

If the lessons take place outdoors it is a good idea to alternate static and mobile practices to keep children warm. It is however a good idea to reserve outdoor lessons for warm days, especially with young children. They find it difficult to concentrate on verbal instruction outdoors for longer than about 12 seconds and therefore often seem to misunderstand what is expected of them when, in fact, they never assimilated the instructions. Initially, they also find the outdoor environment difficult to cope with and need to be introduced gradually to it.

The length of the lessons should vary according to the age of the children. Five-year-olds, for example, can seldom tolerate a lesson which is longer than 15 minutes, yet by the age of seven, children can easily cope with a 30 minute lesson. On the other hand, in some schools the length of the lesson may depend more on the vagaries of timetabling than on the children's developmental stage.

In adult life, games are competitive. I would suggest that the younger the children the less able they are to cope with, or even understand competitive games. The notion of winning or losing is anathema to them. Competitive situations have therefore been reduced to a minimum. Indeed, most of the activities are structured to give every child the chance to participate successfully. Teachers should concentrate on providing an enjoyable environment where children can be encouraged to work together rather than compete against each other. The most important principle of all games teaching as in all aspects of teaching, is to make sure that all the children have a reasonable chance of success.

This may mean organising groups of different abilities to work together, or simply letting friends work together in partner activities, or emphasising and giving praise for improvement rather than for skill ability.

Extra care must be taken with children who have special needs and wherever possible they should be included in the programme of activity. This may mean providing a chair, or adapting the game or shortening the distance so that they can take part.

Many games lessons can seem chaotic because young children often do not have the necessary skills. What they need is practice, not only of ball skills etc, but also in playing together, in learning to share and in learning to move equipment efficiently. All this needs time, patience, and a great deal of repetition. Teachers are encouraged to persevere. Order will come out of the chaos!

Demonstrating skills

The teacher needs to be an accurate observer and a good demonstrator if the children are to be successful at playing games. Each skill must be analysed into the teaching points required and then demonstrated. Children find it much easier to learn when they are shown what to do rather than just given verbal instructions. Teachers must also attempt to give left-handed and left-footed demonstrations since a small percentage of children in each class will be 'left-sided'. The children should be close enough to see and hear at all times. The teacher should consider showing an action or grip from different angles and should draw the children's attention to the specific part of the skill which she wishes to reinforce. They should then be allowed to practise the particular skill as quickly as possible.

In any lesson where children are physically active it is important for the teacher to position himself where he can see the whole class all the time.

Children should be encouraged to analyse their activities. Some questions are suggested in the text. The teacher can add to this question bank as and when the need arises. When social and moral issues arise it is a good idea to try and throw the question back to the children. 'What do you think?' 'What do you suggest we should do about this?' 'Why do you think we should introduce this rule?' etc. This way they can begin to understand the tasks which they have been asked to perform.

At this stage in children's schooling it should not be necessary to draw teachers attention to the care which should be taken about sex-typed curricula or sex differentiation within the curriculum. In class lessons children of primary school age should always be taught in mixed groups. This includes football, netball and cricket! We do have a national women's football and cricket team remember! To exclude girls or boys from any class activity is discriminatory and educationally unsound. Girls and boys are equally strong and equally competent at the primary stage and teachers should prepare curricula which encourage games playing which can be enjoyed together.

Pauline Wetton

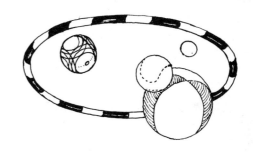

Activities for five year olds

Whistle stop

What you need
Whistle.

Objective
To increase the children's listening skills and give confidence in locomotor activity.

Warming up exercises
Ask the children to walk anywhere. Encourage them to look for spaces. Tell them that when you blow the whistle they should stay still. Repeat several times.

Skill training
Ask the children to run, looking for spaces. On the whistle they must stop still. Repeat.

Gather the children together at one end of the playground. Ask them to walk from one side to the other. After a few times change to running from one side to the other. Try asking them to run across the playground, turn and come back to start. Choose a line for them to turn on.

Game

What time is it Mr Wolf?
You are Mr Wolf. Walk around the area followed by the children who shout 'What time is it Mr Wolf?' You should answer 2 o'clock, then perhaps 6 o'clock until eventually you say 'dinner time'. The children turn and race 'home'. Try to catch the children. If a child is caught he joins you. Continue until all the children have been caught.

Find your spot

What you need
Whistle.

Objective
To increase the children's listening skills and achieve quality in locomotor activity.

Warming up exercises
Start the lesson by letting the children run freely. Call the class together and tell them that you are going to try different ways of walking. Ask them to walk slowly; then quickly – tell them to change on your signal. Let them experiment with walking on their heels; then on their toes. Signal when you wish them to change. Get them to take long strides; then short strides – changing on your signal. Can they suggest any other ways of walking?

Skill training
Tell the children to walk around looking for spaces. On your signal, they must turn and walk in the opposite direction. Try getting them to walk on the lines of the playground. Let them try walking backwards.

Change to running. On your signal they must change direction. Get them to choose their 'own spot' on the playground. Let them run anywhere, and on your signal, run and stand on their 'own spot'.

Game
What time is it Mr Wolf? (see page 7).

Run, skip and hop

What you need
Whistle,
3 coloured bands.

Objective
To practise locomotor activities.

Warming up exercises
Tell the class to run anywhere, stopping on the whistle. Then ask them to hop anywhere. Get them to practice hopping first on one leg, then the other. Use the whistle to signal when they should switch legs.

Ask them to alternate legs when hopping – first on the left, then on the right, etc. Some children may start to skip naturally.

Skill training
Demonstrate how to skip. Let them practise. Ask them to run forwards, then backwards. Alternate the two – signal when they should change.

Ask them to walk; on the whistle they should change to running. When the whistle blows again, they should change back to walking. Repeat several times. Play 'find your spot'. Encourage them to use all the playground.

Game

Stick in the mud
Choose two children to be catchers with you. You each should wear an arm or shoulder band. When the other children are touched they must stand still. The last three children to be caught become the new catchers.

Freeze!

What you need
Whistle,
3 coloured bands.

Objective
To practise locomotor activities and controlled stopping.

Warming up exercises
Ask the children to skip around the playground. Have them hop on the left leg; then on the right leg. Use the words left and right to help them learn the meanings.

Skill training
Have them walk around. On the whistle they must 'freeze'. Emphasise that no movement is allowed. Repeat with running.
   Let them choose their own spot. Signal for them to run away. On your whistle, they should go back to their spot and stand still. Do the same again only this time tell them that on the whistle they have to go and jump on their spot.

Game
Stick in the mud (see page 9).

9

Bean bag toss: 1

What you need
Whistle,
bean bag for each child,
basket.

Objective
To encourage manipulative skills.

Warming up exercises
Have the children run anywhere. Ask them to hop on the left foot, then on the right. Keep signalling for them to change feet. Tell them to skip anywhere. Ask them to try skipping with a high knee lift.

Skill training
Give each child a bean bag. Ask them to walk around the playground balancing it on the palm of the hand, the back of the hand, the head, the shoulder etc. Let the children make other suggestions.

Tell them to throw the bean bag as high as they can and watch it fall. Let them collect their bag on your signal. Try asking them to throw the bean bag as far as they can. Remind them to keep their eyes on the bag. Signal for them to collect it.

Get them to hold the bean bag in front of them, then drop it and pick it up.

Using first the right then the left hand, ask them to run with the bean bag and on the whistle put it down. Tell them to keep looking at it and walk away. Signal for them to pick it up.

Game

Keep the basket full
Throw the bean bags as far away from the basket as possible. The children collect them and try to keep the basket full. You win if you manage to empty the basket.

Bean bag toss: 2

What you need
Whistle,
bean bag for each child,
basket.

Objective
To encourage manipulative skills.

Warming up exercises
Ask the children to run anywhere and 'freeze' when the whistle blows. Repeat several times. Collect the children together and tell them to jump with both feet together, bouncing on the spot. Then ask them to try jumping forwards on two feet, then jumping as high as possible.

Skill training
Let the children run freely. On the whistle get them to bend down and touch the ground. Repeat.

Throw bean bags all over the playground and let each child collect one. Ask the children to run freely. On the whistle they should bend down and put the bag on the floor and carry on running. On the second whistle they should pick up the nearest bag.

Ask the children to throw their bean bag a long way. Remind them to watch where their bag drops. On your signal they should collect it – then walk! Tell them to drop their bag, then pick it up, first using the left hand then the right. Tell them to throw the bag as high as they can using the right hand. Repeat with the left hand. Signal for them to pick it up between throws. Remind them to watch their bag all the time.

Game
Keep the basket full (see page 10).

Two-handed toss

What you need
Large ball for each child.

Objective
To introduce overarm throwing.

Warming up exercises
Tell the children to choose their own spot on the floor and remember it. Let them run anywhere. On your signal they should return to their own spot. Change the rules after a few goes. Tell them that on the signal they should now jump up and down with two feet until asked to stop. Try using different signals for each action; then you can surprise them!

Skill training
Ask the children to toss the ball with two hands into a space, keeping their eyes on their ball. Let them collect it on your command. Now let them try a two-handed toss upwards towards the sky. Encourage them to watch the ball drop. On your command they can pick it up.

Ask the children to squat behind the ball on the floor. Tell them to push until it rolls away. You may need to demonstrate this. Encourage them to watch the ball, and on your command run and pick it up.

Game

Take the ball for a walk
Tell the children to take their ball 'for a walk', by batting it first with the right hand, then with the left hand, to make it roll around the floor. They should try to avoid 'bumping' into each other and look for spaces to move into, moving all the time.

One-handed toss

What you need
Small ball for each child,
10 skittles, whistle,
bean bags.

Objective
To extend the skill of overarm throwing.

Warming up exercises

Statues
Get the children to run anywhere. When you blow the whistle (or equivalent) the children must stop suddenly, hold their position and 'freeze'. Notice if anyone wobbles.

Try asking them to run with very long strides, or very short steps. Ask them to run with their arms outstretched.

Skill training
Let the children practise tossing the ball using only one hand. First ask them to toss the ball into a space. Then suggest that they toss the ball high into the air. Ask them to roll the ball across the ground with one hand (on your signal let them run and collect).

Demonstrate how to throw underarm. Let them practise throwing into a space. Emphasise the necessity to shift the body weight from the back to front foot as they throw.

Accuracy and distance are not important at this stage. Encourage the children to stand sideways; for right-handers the left shoulder should face the line of throw.

Game
Arrange the children in groups of three. Have them stand three steps away from one skittle and practise trying to hit it with a bean bag.
NB If it snows: Build a snowman and aim at him!

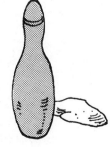

Target practice

What you need
Small ball per child,
10 boxes or baskets,
3 faces.

Objective
To further extend the skill
of overarm throwing.

Warming up exercises

Play statues (see page 13).

Chinese wall
Ask one of the children to stand in the middle of the room.
The rest of the children should stand with their backs to
the wall on one side of the room. On your command they
try to get to the opposite wall. If they are touched by the
middle child they join her in the middle 'on the wall'. The
game continues until everyone is caught.

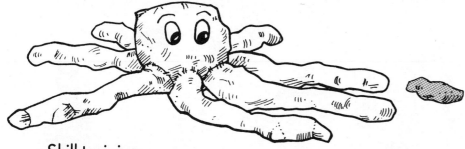

Skill training
Let the children continue to practise throwing the ball
underarm. Keep encouraging them to step on the
opposite foot to the throwing arm. Don't forget to
demonstrate with both the left and the right arm.

Games
Before the games lesson make some targets in the
classroom. Let the children paint faces on large
cardboard boxes with big eyes, nose and mouth. Or they
might like to make stuffed figures to aim at. For example,
an octopus can be made from a body of a pair of tights
and eight legs. The children can stuff the legs with paper
and be helped to sew up the ends. Stuff the body and
attach the legs, then add eyes.

At the games lesson put the targets on chairs. Have the
children practise hitting the nose, the mouth etc.

Alternatively, get the children to practise throwing the
balls into large boxes or baskets from a stated distance
(don't make it too far to begin with).

Kick that ball!

What you need
Large ball per child.

Objective
To introduce the skill of kicking a ball.

Warming up exercises
Ask the children to hop anywhere on one leg. Tell them that when the whistle blows they must change legs. Demonstrate to the class how to skip step. Let them practise first with the right side leading, then with the left side leading.

Have the children leap from one foot to the other. Tell them to try and stay in the air as long as possible.

Skill training
Introduce the skill of kicking in stages. First practise the foot motion. Ask the children to stand on one leg and swing the other one gently forwards and through to behind.

To practise kicking get each child to put a ball on the ground in front of them. The body and ball should be kept still. Ask them to prepare and kick the ball (remind them to watch it and collect on your signal).

The next stage is to practise walking to and kicking a still ball and eventually running to and kicking a still ball. Plenty of practice is essential. They will need practice manipulating the ball with their feet. Suggest they try taking the ball for a walk (see page 12) using their feet only.

Game
Chinese wall (see page 14).

15

Catch it: 1

What you need
Bean bag for
each child,
a basket.

Objective
To introduce the
skill of catching.

Warming up exercises
Let the children run anywhere. On your signal, they
should stop and clap hands. Introduce a new signal upon
which they have to find a partner and clap hands.
Alternate the two signals — surprise them!

Skill training
Make a class circle and give alternate children a bean
bag. Pass the bean bags round the circle.

   Give each child a bag. Let them practise underarm
throwing high in the air. Remind them to keep their eyes
on the bean bag. Do the same again but this time ask
them to reach out and try to touch the bean bag as it falls.

   Ask the children to choose a partner and stand one
arms length away from each other. One partner should
pass the bean bag with the right hand to the other who
collects in her left hand. Repeat.

   Tell them to stand six steps away from their partner.
They should take turns throwing the bean bag to try and
hit their partner around the middle. The partner should try
to catch it.

Game

Bean bag scramble
Throw the bean bags all over the area, and let the
children try to collect as many as possible. This can be
made more difficult by dividing the class into four colour
groups and getting the children to collect their own
colour of bean bag. Alternatively play keep the basket
full (see page 10).

Catch it: 2

What you need
Large sponge ball, coloured band for every 2 children.

Objective
To extend the skill of catching.

Warming up exercises

Catch
Give four children coloured bands to wear. They must try to 'catch' the other children. When someone is touched they must stand still. The last four children to be caught are the winners.

Skill training
Ask the class to form a circle and give alternate children a ball. Pass the balls around the circle.

Ask the children to find a partner and a ball, then find a spot facing each other. The child with the ball holds it with two hands and runs round the other. She then gives the ball to her partner who does the same. Let them try rolling the ball to their partner. Aim! Watch it!

Game

Catch your partner's tail
Divide the class into partners. Each child tucks a coloured band into the back of their waistband. On the word 'go' they must try to catch their partner's tail.

Note
Catching is much more difficult to learn than throwing because of the amount of co-ordination involved. Children have to be able to watch an object as it moves, then move into the 'line' of the throw. They also have to use their hands without looking at them. Some children may also be fearful of the object to be caught. If they are not to react by turning their heads away, then the objects used must be both soft and well known to them. Bean bags are the best objects to catch in these early stages.

Stage 1
Before trying to teach the children how to catch, make sure they have had many hand/arm strengthening exercises using balls. They will need to have had plenty of practise rolling, tossing and giving the ball to a partner across a reachable space. Remind them to 'Use their eyes to track the ball'. Remember that until children can throw reasonably straight, it is very difficult to teach them to catch!

Demonstrate how to catch. Hold your arms in front of the body with your hands palm-upwards and fingers spread. When the ball makes contact with the hands, bend the elbows quickly and pull the ball into the body with the fingers. Tell them to reach out with 'big hands' and 'pull the ball in'.

Stage 2
Continue rolling and collecting practice. Pat-bouncing a ball gives the children the chance to practise watching the path of the moving ball, judging the best interception point and then moving to collect it. Make sure they use both the right and the left hand. Using partners they can bounce the ball to each other. Tell them to 'Use their hand to show their partner where to throw the ball' and to 'be ready to move into the line of the ball if necessary'.

Stations: 1

What you need
Basket,
6 skittles,
18 bean bags,
12 large balls.

Objective
To provide 'stations' where children can practise the skills introduced so far.

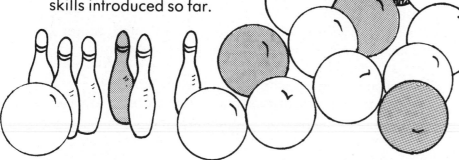

Warming up exercises
Get the children to jump on the spot with both feet together. Let them run anywhere. On a signal, they must stand still and clap hands.

Activities
Divide the class into five groups and ask the children to help you to set up the five 'stations'. Rotate the groups between the stations until everyone has had a turn at each station. You may need to continue the lesson over more than one session. It is useful to make cards for each station to remind the children what to do. List the instructions given here and the equipment required. It is useful to draw a simple diagram of the action required to help those who have difficulty reading. If you cover the cards with clear plastic they will last longer.

Station 1
Basket and 6 bean bags.
Ask the children to practise throwing the bean bags into the basket with an underarm throw.

Station 2
2 skittles and 6 large balls.
Tell the children to practise kicking the ball between the two skittles.

Station 3
6 bean bags.
Ask them to practise throwing the bag underarm as far as possible.

Station 5
2 skittles or faces or other stuffed objects and bean bags.
Let the children practise underarm throwing, aiming to hit the objects.

Station 4
2 skittles and 6 large balls.
Let the children roll the ball between the skittles.

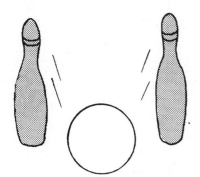

Game

Grandmother's footsteps
Choose one child to face the wall. The other children stand across the room, facing her back. They creep towards the child, who can turn around at any time. Anyone caught moving is asked to go to the start.

19

Activities for six year olds

Stations: 2

What you need
8 skittles,
6 hoops,
15 large balls,
6 bean bags,
a basket.

Objectives
To evaluate the children's skill
levels in locomotor competency,
manipulative competency and
social/managerial skills.

Warming up exercises
Ask the class to walk anywhere, looking for spaces (this
will help you to assess their spatial awareness).

Ask them to run at speed, and on the whistle stop and
stand still (to assess their listening skills and body
management).

Give them skipping, hopping, and jumping activities
(to test their locomotor and body management
competency).

Activities
Stations are a useful way of assessing the skills level of
your children. Use copy page 121 to record your
observations. As stations require the children to work in
groups and take turns, you will be able to assess their
social and management skills as well as their locomotive
and manipulative competency.

Station 1
2 skittles and 6 large balls.
Ask the children to practise kicking the ball between
skittles (kicking skill).

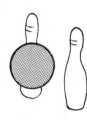

Station 2
3 large balls.
Get the children to roll a ball along the ground to a
partner. The partner should throw it back underarm
(rolling, throwing, catching).

Station 3
Basket and 6 bean bags.
The children should practise underarm throwing into the basket (throwing, aiming).

Station 4
6 skittles (or other objects) and 6 large balls.
Ask them to practise kicking or rolling the ball towards the skittles to try to knock them down (kicking and rolling for precision).

Station 5
6 hoops.
Have them practise jumping over the hoop (jumping).

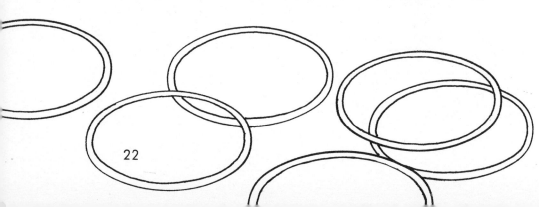

It may take two or even three lessons to complete the evaluation, depending on the time available. After evaluating the children's skill levels it may be necessary to repeat some of the work covered in the previous chapter. You may find that all the children need practice with some skills, eg catching, or it might only be necessary to help certain children who have not yet achieved a particular skill. In the second case it is possible to carry out 'remedial' help by creating skill groups. The children could either work alongside their peers, by adapting the activities of those already 'skilled', or work in a separate group, whilst the other children adapt their work.

The following adaptations can be made for 'skilled' groups:

Station 1
Narrow the gap between the skittles.

Station 2
Throw and catch a smaller ball.

Station 3
Lengthen the distance from the basket.

Station 4
Lengthen the distance from the skittles.

Station 5
Arrange the hoops in pairs so they run and jump over the first hoop, then the second hoop. This will enable you to spend time helping individual children.

Game
Stick in the mud (see page 9).

Bean bag games

What you need
Bean bag per child.

Objectives
To encourage the children to be ambidextrous, to improve hand, eye and foot and eye focus, and to encourage total body use.

Warming up exercises
Let the children skip around the room freely. On your command they must change direction. Re-teach the skip step (see page 15). Let them practise, first with the right side leading, then the left side leading.

Activities
The activities below are listed in order of skill difficulty. Choose as many as are needed to fill the time available.

- Balance the bean bag on your palm and walk around the room. Now use the back of the hand.
- Hold the bag in the right hand. Run backwards and forwards.
- Do the same with the left hand.
- Put the bag on the floor, jump over it, pick it up. Repeat.
- Balance the bag on different parts of the body: head, back, shoulder, foot, etc.
- Try the previous activity whilst walking.
- Try the previous activity whilst running.
- Hold the bag under the chin, under the arm pit, between the knees, between the ankles, between the feet. (Ask the class for suggestions).

23

- Try the previous activity whilst moving, walking, running?
- Put the bag on the floor. Try picking it up with the toes, the inside of the elbow joint, chin and chest etc.
- Sit down. Put the bean bag between your feet. Toss it into the air.
- Toss the bag into a space, watch it drop, collect it. (Sometimes high above the body, sometimes forwards away from the body).

Partner activities
- Stand back to back. Pass the bean bag over your head to your partner. Pass the bag to your partner between the legs. Pass the bag around the sides of her body.
- Sit 2 metres away from your partner. Practise tossing the bag gently and catching it.
- Stand 2 metres away from your partner. Throw the bag underarm to land at your partner's feet.
- One partner holds the hoop at shoulder height. The other has two turns to throw bean bags through the hoop. Collect the bags. Change places.

- Practise tossing with two hands.
- Practise tossing with one hand – alternate right and left.
- Practise throwing. Use targets to help focusing. (Remind them to transfer their weight from the back leg to the front and to follow through the motion.)
- Throw the bag underarm as high as you can in the air. See how many times you can clap before the bag lands.

- Stand 2 metres from your partner. Practise underarm throwing and catching. Aim for your partner's chest. (Stress that they must keep an eye on the bag and move their body into the line of the throw to catch the bag. Encourage them to 'reach out' and 'pull in'. Re-teach the throwing action if necessary.)

Game
Bean bag scramble (see page 16).

Ball games

What you need
Coloured braid per child,
large sponge ball per child
(progressing to smaller and harder balls
when the children are confident and able).

Objective
To improve the children's hand-eye, ball skills.

Warming up exercise
Play tag. Give each child a braid to tuck into the back of
their waistband. Each child should try to catch as many
braids as possible.

Skill training
The activities below have been divided by skill. Spread
the lesson over several sessions, choosing one or two
skills to focus on each time. Give the children plenty of
time to practise.

General ball handling experience
Give each child a large sponge ball. Tell them to hold it
cupped in both hands and let the ball roll down their
arms to the chest. Let them try rolling the ball all over
their body.

Have them stand with their legs apart and weave the
ball around ankles using both hands. Ask them to try
again using just one hand.

Ask them to balance the ball on as many parts of the
body as possible. Let them make suggestions. Ask them
to walk around the area while balancing the ball.

Get the children to roll the ball along the floor by
batting it with their hands. Can they think of any other
way of rolling it along, eg can they roll it along using
their nose?

Catching

Ask the children to throw the ball and try to get it to land as near to their feet as possible. Get them to increase the height thrown each time. When they are able to get the ball to land relatively consistently close to their feet, ask them to catch it with both hands, pulling the ball into the body.

Pre-volleyball skills

Show the class how to hit the ball, volleyball style. Throw the ball up, when it reaches chest level on the way down bat it back up with hands cupped together, palms uppermost. Let them practise.

Bouncing

Ask the children to drop the ball and see how high they can get it to come back up. Tell them to bounce the ball back each time it comes up using both hands. Let them try using only one hand, alternating hands each time.

Ask the children to run across the area holding the ball without dropping it. Give everyone a hoop and ask them to place it somewhere in the area. Ask them to run with their ball. When you clap they must find the nearest hoop and bounce the ball inside it (while standing outside it). Repeat many times.

Throwing

Demonstrate the overarm throw again. Remind them to transfer their weight from the back foot to the front, rocking from their heels to their toes. Show them how to hold the ball in one hand, keeping the feet together and the arm back. Move the whole body together. As you move your hand forward to throw the opposite leg moves forward. Let go of the ball when the arm is in front and follow through with the rest of the body so that you carry on moving forward. Let them practice.

If you have a wall, get the children to practise throwing against it. Alternatively line up some skittles for them to knock down.

Games

Makes lines of four, with the children standing one behind the other. Have each child pass the ball over his own head to the person behind without turning. The fourth person runs to the front with the ball and everyone moves back one pace.

Try doing the same, but with passing the ball between the legs.

Hoopla!

What you need
A hoop for each child,
20 obstacles.

Objectives
To encourage manual dexterity
and hand-eye co-ordination.

Warming up exercises
Give each child a hoop and ask them to place it
somewhere on the floor. Let them run anywhere outside
the hoops until you call 'home'. They should then run and
stand in their hoop.

Get the children to run round the outside of their hoop
clockwise. Repeat going anti-clockwise.

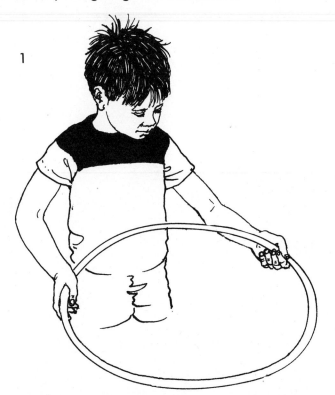

1

Activities
Give the children plenty of opportunities to get used to
playing with the hoops, first holding it horizontally (1),
then vertically (2).

2

Tell them to thread the hoop over the head, body, legs
and step out. Do the reverse. Ask them to jump into the
hoop, lift it, thread it up the body, over the head and put it
on the floor again. Get them to move around the room
using this pattern.

Ask the children to hold the hoop around their waist
and run around the room. Have them spin the hoop on
the floor using both hands. They should try to keep the
hoop vertical as long as possible. Let them practise
rolling the hoop into a space. When it stops they can
collect it. Ask them to try to keep the hoop rolling by
using a forward motion of the hand. See if the can 'skip'
with the hoop. Let them practise.

Games
- Hoops (see page 102).
- Put bean bags or skittles as obstacles and let the
  children practise bowling the hoops in and out of the
  obstacles.

Skipping ropes

What you need
A rope for each child.

Objective
To teach the children how to skip with a rope.

Warming up exercises
Ask the class to jump on the spot with two feet together. Then let them skip around the room freely. Now ask them to jump on the spot with both feet together and their arms stretched out at shoulder height.

Activities
Give each child a rope and ask them to place it on the floor in a straight line. Let them practise walking on the rope. Ask them to walk from one end to the other with the left foot on one side of the rope and the right foot on the other. Now have them hop on one foot alongside the rope keeping as near to the rope as possible. Ask them to try with the other foot.

Ask them to fold the rope in half. Holding the two ends together let them practise swinging and circling the rope in the space, first with one hand and then the other.

Ask the children to swing the shortened rope like a pendulum first with their right hand and then their left.

Have them open the rope and hold an end in each hand. Ask them to practise swinging the rope in a pendulum movement from the front to the back of the body, jumping over the rope so that it swings under their feet.

Skill training
Teach the skipping action. Show them how to hold the rope at shoulder height, with the arms stretched wide and the elbows slightly bent. The rope should fall behind the body with the loop resting just above heel height. Keep the arms wide, turn the rope over the head, and jump over it as it swings forward towards the feet. Give them plenty of time to practise.

Games
See skipping games on page 111.

29

Kicking fun

What you need
A large ball
for each child.

Objectives
To increase the children's ability to bounce, kick and
dribble a large ball.

Warming up exercises
Ask the children to hold the ball in the palm of the hand
and balance it without using the fingers. See if they can
walk around the room without dropping it. Play 'Take the
ball for a walk' (see page 12). Try using the feet instead
of the hands.

Get the children to stand with their legs astride and use
their hands to roll the ball around the feet and between
the legs in a figure eight.

Activities
Ask the children to hold the ball resting on both palms.
Then drop and catch it. Ask them to let go with one hand
and pat bounce the ball, then catch it.

Ask them to pat bounce the ball near the body. Then
ask them to try and walk whilst pat bouncing the ball.

Re-teach the children how to kick the ball (see page
15). Give them plenty of opportunity to practise.

Tell the children to place the ball between their ankles.
Holding the ball tightly, ask them to try to walk. Let them
practise dribbling, first using their insteps, then using the
outside of the foot. Encourage them to use small, easy
kicks. Ask them to dribble the ball with their hands, first
using the right and then the left. Let them experiment with
different ways of dribbling, eg batting the ball, punching
the ball with a fist, pushing the ball with the palm of the
hand, etc.

Ask them to toss the ball into the air, let it drop and
bounce and then catch it with both hands.

Game
Divide the class into groups. Let the children take turns
dribbling the ball around the group. Do the same, but
using the hand. Then try pat bouncing using either or
both hands.

30

Ball handling: 1

What you need
Small sponge ball
for each child.

Objectives
To increase manual dexterity
and hand-eye co-ordination.

Warming up exercise

Follow my leader
Divide the class into twos. One child chooses what action
to do: eg walk, run, skip, hop, jump etc. The second child
should follow behind and copy whatever the leader does.

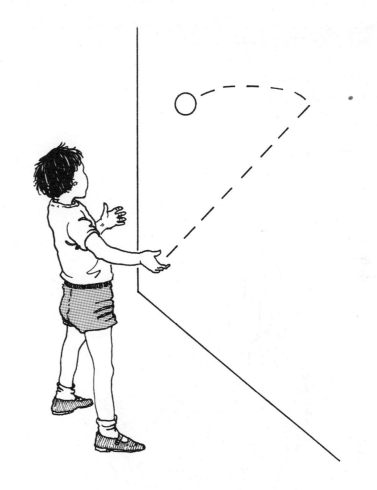

Skill training
Play the ball games on pages 25–27 using small balls.

Activities
Practise underarm throwing and catching the ball against
a wall. Tell them to throw the ball, let it bounce, then
catch it. Ask them to try throwing and catching the ball
without letting it bounce. They may need to stand closer
to the wall.

Batting practice

What you need
A bat and
a small ball
for each child,
a basket,
5 containers.

Objective
To teach batting skills.

Warming up exercise

Trains
Ask the children to find a partner. Get them to stand one behind the other, with the child behind holding their partner's waist. Then ask them to practise stopping, starting, running, walking, etc by command.

Skill training
Let each child hold the bat in whichever hand he prefers. Encourage them to complete the following movements whilst holding the bat tightly:

- Reach high above your head.
- Reach out to the right/the left.
- Touch your right foot/left foot.
- Hold the bat with the elbow bent.
- Practise twisting the wrist to the right/left.
- Practise tipping the wrist forward then back.
- Practise bending the arm at the elbow then straightening it.
- Hold the bat wide with a straight arm.
- Practise swinging the arm from low to high with a smooth upward sweep.

Encourage the children to move their feet, particularly when swinging.

Ask the children to balance a ball on their bat. Get them to practise walking while trying to keep the ball balanced on the bat. Let them practise pat bouncing the ball upwards. Encourage them to try to stay standing in one spot. Suggest that they count how many times they can pat it before it drops'. 'Two?' 'Three?.

Ask them to bat the ball along the floor. Encourage them to keep the ball near to the bat. Have them put the bat on top of the ball and practise moving the ball in a small space.

Ask them to bat the ball as far away as possible. Tell them to watch where it goes, collect it and come back to the place where they started.

Game
Divide the class into five colour groups, and give each group a container. Start with all the balls in a basket. Roll the balls over the area. Get the children to run and field them and take them back to their group's container. They then count how many they have collected.

Activities for seven year olds

Stations: 3

What you need
9 small balls,
15 large balls,
6 skipping ropes,
3 baskets or boxes,
6 skittles.

Objectives
To evaluate the children's skill levels.
- General mobility, suppleness, stamina.
- Co-ordination of gross motor skills.
- Co-ordination and control of finer motor skills.
- Listening ability – task completion.
- Social/managerial skills.

Warming up exercises
Give the children a chance to run, skip and hop freely. Signal when you want them to change. Ask the children to jump 30 times on the spot with both feet together. Then ask them to run at top speed across the area ten times.

Give the children stretching exercises to help them to supple up. Ask them to stand and stretch up high, holding their hands out wide, then curl up, still on their feet. From standing, get them to bend at the waist and flop forwards. Ask them to 'circle' their wrists, shoulders, ankles, hips, etc to loosen up.

Activities
Set up the following six stations to challenge the skill level of all the children. Get them to rotate in groups around each station until everyone has had a turn. Fill in the evaluation sheet (see photocopiable page 122) as they are going round. These evaluation sheets are an important record of the children's ability.

Station 1
3 boxes or baskets,
6 (or more) small balls.
Throw the ball underarm into a container. Take a step away from the container each time a successful throw is completed.

Station 2
3 large balls.
Practise throwing underarm and catching with a partner.

Station 3
3 small balls.
The same activity as for Station 2.

Station 4
6 skittles,
6 large balls.
Practise kicking the ball to knock down a skittle. Each time a skittle falls take a step away from the skittle.

Station 5
6 large balls.
Ask the children to count how many times they can pat bounce the ball in succession.

Station 6
6 skipping ropes.
Practise skipping. Ask the children to count how many skips they can do without stopping.

After the evaluation sheet is complete, you will be able to decide which activities need further practice and introduce suitable lessons from the earlier chapters. If only certain children need extra help, set up stations. By varying the challenges you will be able to stretch them while allowing the less competent more time to practise under your supervision.

Bean bag clap

What you need
Bean bag
for each child.

Objectives
To increase the children's
perceptual awareness and
fine motor control.

Warming up exercise

Fly in the room
Tell the class that there is a fly in the room and they have
to catch it – but only you know where it is. Give the
children directions, eg 'in that corner', 'no, that corner',
'look up high', 'look down low', etc.

Skill training
Ask the children to put a bean bag on their head, tip it off
and catch it as it drops. Ask them to toss the bag from the
right hand to the left and vice versa. Tell them to throw the
bag high and catch it high, then catch it low. Get them to
try this whilst sitting or kneeling.
 Ask them to throw the bag high in the air, clap once
and catch it. See how many times they can clap before
catching it. 'Twice?' 'Three times?'
 Let them experiment. Can they clap between their legs
between throws? Or behind their backs? Ask them to try
to turn round once before catching. Can they touch
their toes in between throws? How about their knees and
toes, or head and toes?
 Let them try to think of different ways of throwing the
bag around the back, from under the leg, etc. Let them
practise batting the bean bag with the hand.

Game
Keep the basket full (see page 10).

37

Catching and fielding

What you need
A small ball (tennis size) per child,
a skittle between two children.

Objectives
To reinforce throwing, catching and fielding skills.

Warming up exercises

Spiders and sparrows
Have all the children line up at one side of the area, then crouch down with their hands on the floor and their backs to the way they are going. On a given signal they should move backwards on their feet and hands. When they get to the other side they should stand up and hop back to the start on one leg.

Skill training

Catching
Ask the children to throw the ball underarm, high into the air. They should watch the flight of the ball and move the body *if necessary*, so that it is underneath the ball. Tell them to reach up with both hands to meet the ball, and draw the ball into the body. Encourage them to keep their wrists and elbows flexible and to give with their hands when they are catching.

Throwing
Let them practise overarm throwing by aiming at targets. When using small balls they should be encouraged to hold the ball with the fingers and to flick the wrist. Watch to see that they are transferring their weight and following through with their body.

Fielding
As soon as the ball is released they should watch where it goes, and on a given signal, chase after it to pick it up and run back to their starting place.

Let them choose partners. Get one to roll the ball along the ground (strongly and with speed). The other should try to stop the ball by getting behind or in line with it. Tell them to crouch down, keeping their heels together, with the palms of both hands facing the oncoming ball, ready to catch it. Eventually, this should merge into one continuous action. Progress to lunging to the right or left to field the ball with one hand when necessary. Carry on using a wall. The ball will rebound quicker and help to encourage quick reflexes.

Game
In pairs, they should take turns trying to knock down a skittle. The non thrower retrieves the ball.

Balls and hoops

What you need
A small ball per child,
a hoop between two.

Objective
To increase the
children's ball skills.

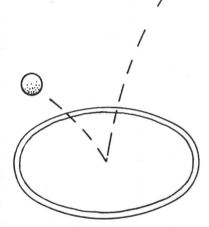

Warming up exercises
Tell the children to jump on the spot with both feet together until you say 'Change'. They can then run anywhere – repeat.

Butterfly touch
Let the children choose partners. One child should stand facing a wall with his hands behind his back. The other should creep from across the playground to touch the partner's hands. As soon as he makes the touch he races back to his starting position. If the other child can catch him he wins.

Skill training
Divide the class into twos. Ask each pair to place a hoop an equal distance between them. Have the children practise throwing the ball underarm, to land in the hoop and be fielded by their partner. Do the same but this time have them practise bouncing the ball into the hoop for their partner to catch.

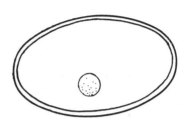

Ask the children to practise walking and pat bouncing the ball. Tell them to walk and toss the ball a little way into the air and catch it. Do the same with running.

Give the children underarm bowling practise with targets. Encourage the children to pitch the ball straight. The action should be slow, easy and flowing. Have the children start near to the target. Accuracy should come first, then distance.

Working in pairs, let them practise first underarm then overarm bowling and catching.

Games
Have races between two lines. Here are some ideas:

- Run as fast as you can.
- Hop on your left leg.
- Hop on your right leg.
- Go as fast as you can while pat bouncing a ball.
- Dribble a ball with your hand.
- Roll the ball along to the line and field it back.

Batting skills: 1

What you need
A bat and a small ball
for each child,
6 hoops (4 colours),
4 children for each hoop.

Objective
To teach the skill of batting.

Warming up exercises
Spread the hoops around the area. Ask the children to run anywhere. When you give a signal they must choose a hoop to stand in (four children maximum). When they are all inside a hoop, call out a colour, eg yellow. All the children in that colour hoop have 'lost'. Repeat.

Skill training
Let the children practise a few ball handling skills first, eg bouncing, rolling, catching, bowling, etc. They should also practise bat handling (see page 32) and pat bouncing the ball upwards. Ask them to throw the ball in the air and collect it on the bat, or let it bounce and collect it on the rebound with the bat.

Have the children throw the ball against the wall, let it bounce, then bat it back towards the wall.

Divide the class into pairs. The batter should stand sideways to the bowler, with the left shoulder leading (for right handers), the feet about shoulder width apart ('comfortable') and the body 'ready'. The bat should be held out to the side in line with and a little below shoulder level (although at first it is easier for beginners to start with the bat held back behind their bodies). Using more or less the same shoulder action as if she were throwing the ball over arm the batter should swing the bat easily backward, then forward with as strong an action as possible to hit the ball. The body weight should swing forward at the same time as the bat swings forward.

Encourage the batter from the beginning to:

- Open her shoulders.
- Attack the ball.
- Let the arm, shoulder and body co-ordinate into one flowing action.
- Hit the ball rather than patting or pushing it.
- Put body weight behind the hitting action.

Game

Short tennis
Set up two 'nets'. If it is possible, use padder tennis posts and nets, if not, try and rig a rope between two posts. Divide the children into pairs, two pairs at each net. Each pair should use the same kind of bat. The server must bounce the ball and hit it across 'the net' to start the game. The receiver must let the ball bounce once before hitting it back over 'the net'.

Encourage co-operation. The aim of the game is to see how many consecutive successful returns can be made over the net. Ask for scores after about five minutes. Let the pair with the highest number of consecutive returns, show the rest of the class how they have been successful.

Batting skills: 2

What you need
Table tennis bats and ball.
Badminton raquets and shuttlecocks.
Squash rackets and balls (junior size).
Short tennis bats and ball.
Cricket bats and tennis balls (junior size).
Play bats and sponge balls.
Battington, etc.

Objective
To give further practice in batting skills.

Warming up exercises
Choose a game to play from the five minute fillers chapter (see pages 98–107).

Activities
Give the class as much experience as possible using raquets and bats. Ideally they should have the opportunity to play with all the bats listed in Basic Equipment (see page 126).

Games
Have four games for the children, two of French cricket and two of short tennis (see page 41).

French cricket
One child uses a cricket bat to 'protect' his legs. He must stay on one spot. The other children can move to field the ball but must stay in one place to aim. The fielders try to hit the legs of the batsman. If a child hits the batsman's legs that child becomes the batsman.

Practice stations

What you need
3 coloured braids,
9 skipping ropes,
2 large balls,
11 skittles,
3 canes, 3 baskets,
3 small balls, bean bags.

Warming up exercises
Give three children braids to carry. They have to chase and touch other children. When someone is touched they should take the braid and become a 'catcher'. When you stop the game, ask which children have never been touched. They are the winners.

Activities
Divide the children into groups (the number of children in a group will depend on the space available). Working in stations will give individual children the chance to practise various skills.

Station 1
6 skipping ropes.
Let the children practise skipping with a rope.

Station 2
2 large balls,
2 skittles and a rope.
Ask the children to stand behind a line then kick the ball between the skittles. They should take turns at being the goal keeper.

Station 3
3 skittles, 3 tennis balls and a rope.
Have the children work in pairs to practise underarm bowling by trying to hit the skittle. Let half the children be fielders. They should roll the ball back to the bowler. Let the bowler have four turns then change places.

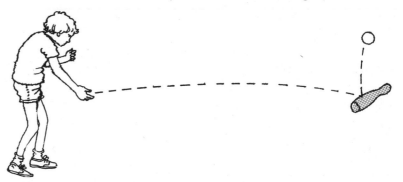

Station 4
3 canes and 6 skittles.
Set up the skittles and canes as shown. Ask the children to take turns jumping over the canes.

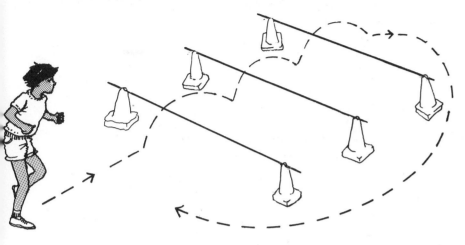

Station 5
3 baskets,
plenty of bean bags, a rope.
Have the children practise underarm throwing into the basket from standing behind the rope.

It is easy to vary the stations to enable the children to practise particular skills. Here are some more ideas:

- Ask the children to take turns running around the skittles as shown. Encourage them to practise turning quickly.

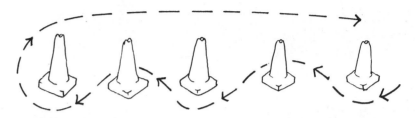

- Place four hoops in a row on the ground. Get the children to practise running and jumping over the hoops. Let the children practise pat bouncing a tennis ball into and out of the hoops, or around and between them.

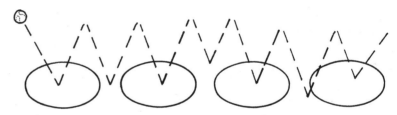

- Ask the children to practise hopping sideways, first with the left foot and then the right foot. Use hoops or lines to hop between.

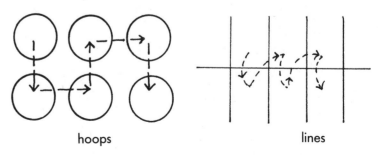

hoops   lines

Activities for eight to nine year olds

Stations: 4

What you need
6 skipping ropes,
14 large balls,
6 small balls,
hoops and skittles.

Objective
To evaluate the children's skill levels.

Warming up exercises
Tell the children to jog on the spot 100 times. Ask them to stretch their arms high above the head, stretching the whole body, standing on tiptoes. Make them hold this position for five seconds. Repeat five times.

Let the children jog anywhere. Shout 'change', when you want them to start sprinting. When you say 'change' a second time they should revert to jogging. Repeat ten times.

Activities
Set up six stations to challenge the skill level of all the children. Get them to rotate in groups around each station until everyone has had a turn. Fill in the evaluation sheet (see copy page 123) as they are going round.

Station 1
6 skipping ropes.
Get the children to practise skipping with a rope. They should count the largest number of consecutive skips.

Station 2
6 large balls.
Ask the children to pat bounce the ball with either hand. Ask them to count how many times the ball is bounced successively.

45

Station 3
4 skittles and 2 large balls.
Set up the skittles as shown. Let them take turns
dribbling the ball in and out of the skittles with their feet.

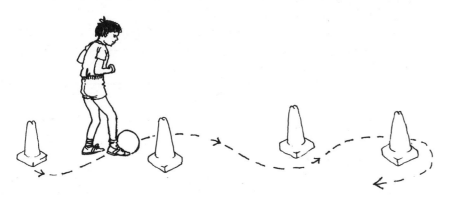

Station 4
3 hoops and 3 large balls.
One child should hold a hoop at shoulder height.
Another child should be the fielder. Ask them to take turns
throwing a large ball underarm through the hoop. The
fielder should roll the ball back to the next player.

Station 5
3 large balls.
Divide the class into twos or threes. Ask the children to
stand 3 metres apart. Have them practise overarm
throwing (from the shoulder) and catching using a large
ball.

Station 6
6 small balls.
Ask the children to throw underarm a small ball up in the
air and catch it.

After the evaluation sheet is complete you will be able
to assess which activities need further practice. Choose
activities from the previous chapter where necessary.

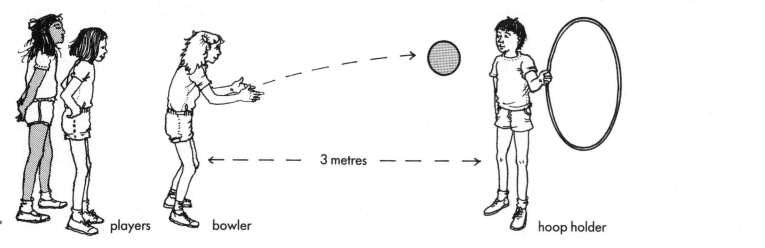

players   bowler   3 metres   hoop holder   fielder

Ball skills: 1

What you need
A large ball each.

Objective
To give further teaching
and practice to individual
children in ball handling skills.

Warming up exercise
Ask the children to jog on the spot, then anywhere
in the space. Ask them to try jogging backwards.

Skill training
Get the children to put the ball on the palm of the hand
and pat it up in the air. Ask them to pat bounce the ball on
to the floor, using first the left hand and then the right
hand.

Re-teach throwing the ball up in the air. Have the
children practise throwing the ball straight upwards. Tell
them to let the ball bounce, then catch it with both hands.

Ask them to pat bounce the ball with one hand and
take a walk on the bounce. Tell them to keep changing
from the left to the right hand.

Ask the children to find a partner and put one ball
away. Get them to stand 3 metres apart, and practise
underarm and overarm throwing and catching. Tell them
to bounce the ball for their partner to catch. Ask them to
take turns pat bouncing the ball around each other. Have
them throw the ball to their partner when changing turns.

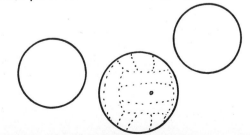

Notes
Encourage the children to reach for the ball when they
are catching. The arms and hands should be stretched
out to meet the oncoming ball. Explain to the class that
they will need to reach in the direction of the ball:
sometimes upwards, sometimes outwards and sometimes
they may need to bend for a low ball, dropping their
hands as necessary.

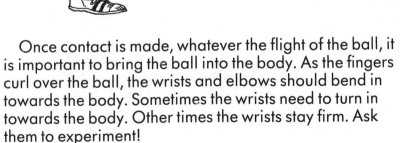

Once contact is made, whatever the flight of the ball, it
is important to bring the ball into the body. As the fingers
curl over the ball, the wrists and elbows should bend in
towards the body. Sometimes the wrists need to turn in
towards the body. Other times the wrists stay firm. Ask
them to experiment!

Game

Team passing rounders (4 large balls)

Make a square formation with four teams. The person in the middle throws underarm to player 1. Player 1 throws the ball back to the middle. Each player has a turn until player 7. When the middle person has thrown to player 7, player 7 catches the ball, holds it tight and runs around the square and back to his own team. He stands in player 1's place and everyone else moves up. Player 7 (now player 1) throws the ball to the person in the middle. The game ends when all the team have had a turn at being player 7. In another lesson at a later stage this game can be adapted by using: a shoulder pass, a chest pass, a kick (soccer), a drive or push pass (hockey), or a smaller ball.

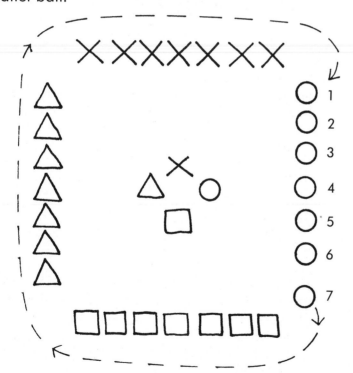

Kick and dribble

What you need
A large ball each,
21 skittles or markers.

Objective
To increase the children's ability to kick and dribble a large ball.

Warming up exercises
Ask the children to jog anywhere in the space. On your whistle or command, get the children to bend and touch the floor and then continue jogging.

Have them stand with their legs wide apart. Ask them to jump diagonally onto the right and then the left foot moving forwards. Repeat going backwards.

Get the children to do little running steps on the spot. Ask them to run anywhere. On your whistle they should change to little quick running steps on the spot. Repeat.

Skill training

If there are not enough balls to go around have the children play in twos and threes.

Let the children practise moving the ball with their feet. Ask them which part of the foot allows better control of the ball. Get them to try different parts of the foot, eg the toe, the outside, the inside. Make them use both feet. Ask them 'Which foot do you like to use more? Why?' Encourage them to use both feet alternately.

Ask them to choose partners and stand 3 metres apart. Tell them to dribble the ball to their partner and then run back to own place.

Still in twos have one child stand with his legs wide apart. His partner kicks the ball between his legs, then sprints to collect it. They should take turns.

Divide the class into fours. Player 1 dribbles the ball around the others players as shown. Player 2 then moves to player 1's place and player 1 runs to player 4's place. Continue until everybody has had a turn.

Ask the class 'How much power do you need to make the ball move along the ground? Which part of the foot should you use?'

'What do you have to do with your eyes and your body to make the ball go straight?'

Game

Divide the class into teams of four. Three should be strikers, and the fourth the goalkeeper. Set up two skittles for a goal. Place a third about 3 metres in front of it. Have the players dribble from about 5 metres away to the front skittle and then shoot at goal.

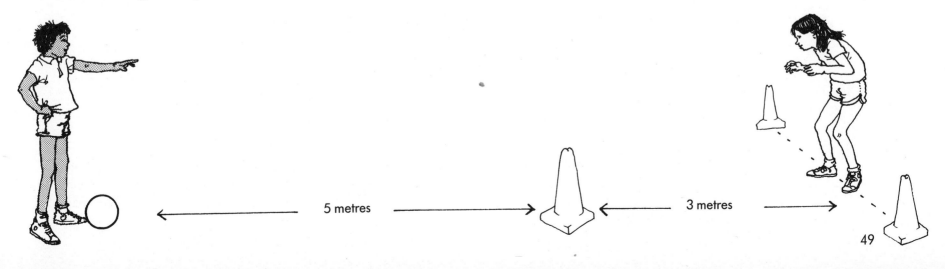

5 metres   3 metres

49

Ball skills: 2

What you need
A large ball
for each child,
a hoop between
2 children.

Objectives
To increase the children's pre-basketball
and pre-volleyball skills.

Warming up exercises
Tell the children that they should face you all the time.
Ask them to walk forwards, backwards, sideways to the
left, sideways to the right, etc. You will be able to test the
children's listening reaction time by saying 'forwards, to
the left, forwards, backwards' etc.

Ask the children to skip lifting the left knee high, then
the right knee high. Get them to skip as high as possible.

Tell them to run and jump high in the air with one arm
held high, then with two arms held high.

Skill training
Tell the children to put the ball on the palms of both
hands and practise patting the ball into the air. Ask them
to try to make at least three successive pats.

Using first one hand then the other, ask them to dribble
the ball around the body using a basketball pat bounce.
Tell them they can move the feet and body as necessary,
but that they should try to 'face' the same way all the
time.

Partner activities
Have the children take turns bouncing the ball into a
hoop. Tell them to use the right hand, then the left and
then both. The partner should reach out to catch the ball.

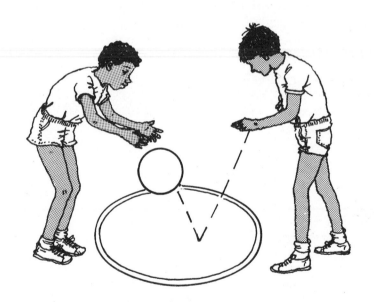

Get them to take turns bouncing the ball around a
hoop using the right hand. Repeat using the left hand.

Ask the children to keep the ball in the air as long as
possible. They should take it in turns to pat the ball.

3   1   2   4

Game
Divide the class into groups of four or six. Player 1 should pat bounce the ball to player 2 and then run to stand behind player 4. Player 2 pat bounces the ball to player 3 and waits. Then player 3 pat bounces the ball to player 4 and waits. Player 4 pat bounces the ball to player 2 and so on until everybody is back 'home'.

Working in groups of four or six, have the children try to keep the ball in the air for as long as possible. No child may have two successive pats of the ball.

Batting and bowling

What you need
A small ball and
bat with a short handle
for each child,
a yellow band,
a blue band.

Objective
To increase the children's batting and bowling skills.

Warming up exercises

Frost and sun
Give one child a blue band and another a yellow band. All the children should move around the area. If they are touched by the catcher with a blue band they should 'freeze'. The player with a yellow band is the only person who is able to unfreeze them.

Skill training
Tell the children to use the flat of their hand as a bat and try to pat the ball into the air ten times without letting it bounce. Ask the class, 'What should you do with your feet? How important are your eyes?'

Ask them to pat the ball with the flat of the hand, then with the back of the hand. Ask them, 'Why is this more difficult?' Ask them to try to bounce the ball with the side of the hand. Tell them to try using first one side then the other.

Ask the children to try the above activities using a bat. Remind them to keep the wrist firm.

Have the children pat bounce the ball with a bat on the spot. Tell them to try to push the ball downwards, not forwards or sideways. Ask them to pat bounce the ball with a bat whilst walking in the area. Suggest that they try to turn the wrist over. Ask them, 'Which is easier?'

Get the children to pat bounce the ball whilst standing. Without stopping the ball moving ask them to try to kneel down, and then stand up again. Ask them to try to pat bounce the ball with their eyes closed.

Ask the children to drop the ball, let it bounce, then bat it. Get them to try using the right hand, the left hand, forehand and backhand. Tell them to keep the bounces at waist height and near to the body.

Let the children choose partners. Have them roll the ball to each other, standing 5 metres away.

Divide the class into groups of four. Two of them should stand in the middle with their legs apart. The other two should roll the balls between their partner's legs using one hand only. They should co-ordinate the rolling and be ready to move to retrieve the other person's ball. Change places and repeat.

With two bowlers, one fielder and one person holding a hoop as shown below, get the children to practise underarm bowling.

Game
Divide the class into fours to practise batting and bowling. Have a batsman, bowler, backstop and a fielder. Start by letting the ball bounce before batting it.

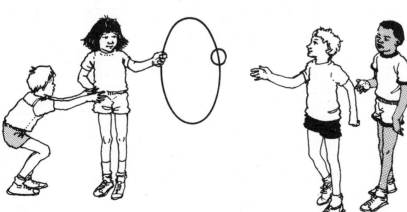

More batting skills

What you need
A bat and
a small ball
for each child,
a hoop between
2 children.

Objective
To continue to increase the children's batting skills.

Warming up exercises
Let the children have free practice with a bat and ball.

Skill training
Ask the children to run as fast as possible. On the whistle they must change to skipping. Repeat. Have the children jog forwards. On the whistle they should change to sideways slip steps. Repeat.

Get the children to pat bounce the ball with the bat. Have them pat the ball down on the floor, then into the air. Ask the class, 'Can you do it alternately?' 'Can you use your other hand?' 'Which is easier? Why?'

Let them practise dropping the ball and batting it into a space.

Partner activities

One child should drop the ball into the hoop for the other to bat. Encourage them to bat the ball gently. The first child should try to catch the ball. Get them to stand further and further away from the hoop.

They should try to keep a rally going. One child should start by bouncing the ball to the other who bats it back gently. The first child should then let it bounce and gently bat it back. This is difficult to achieve at this stage. It is more successful if practised against a wall.

Game

French tag

Choose four children to be catchers (a catcher to eight children). The four catchers should try to tag the free players on a low part of their body. The players tagged must hold that part of their body with one hand and try to tag another player in order to become free again.

Notes

When using a bat the wrist should be kept firm. The bat face should point in the direction being aimed at, ie when batting towards a partner, the bat face should face the partner.

If the ball is bouncing too high, wait for it to drop. If the ball is bouncing very low, you will need to bend your knees! If the ball is too close to the body, move away. If it is too far away, move the feet so that you are closer.

Ball handling: 2

What you need
A large ball per child.

Objective
To increase the children's ball handling skills.

Warming up exercises
Let the children skip anywhere. Ask them to try to skip in time with a partner. Play follow my leader (page 31).

Skill training
Have the class practise throwing the ball in the air and catching it. Encourage them to throw higher and higher.

Ask the children to toss the ball in the air and catch it on the back of the hands. Let them try throwing the ball under their leg and then catching it. Ask them to throw the ball in the air, touch their feet, then catch it.

Ask the children to toss the ball, let it rebound on their head and then catch it. Encourage them to lean back and use their forehead.

Ask them to bat the ball from one hand to the other. Have them throw the ball high overhead. Ask them to count how many times they can clap their hands before catching it.

Demonstrate how to do a shoulder pass. Hold the ball with two hands, on the shoulder. Turn sideways as you put your weight on the back foot. Thrust the whole body into the throwing action. Step on to the front foot at the same time as the arm moves forward with the ball. Let the body follow. Let the children practise. Encourage them to watch the ball. Signal for them to retrieve it. Asking the children to step into a hoop as they throw will encourage them to move their body forward.

Partner activities

Stand 3 metres apart, practise underarm throwing and then overarm throwing. Let them experiment. Ask them, 'Which kind of throw is more successful for an accurate low pass? A straight pass? A high pass?'

Game

Pig in the middle

Ask the children to stand in lines of three. The two outside children throw the ball to each other. If the 'pig' in the middle catches it, he takes the thrower's place. Ask the children, 'What do you have to do to intercept the ball?' 'How can the thrower make sure that the receiver gets the ball?' 'What does the receiver have to do?'

Aiming skills

What you need
9 large balls,
10 small balls,
2 bean bags,
5 hoops, 7 skittles,
2 chairs, a bench,
a basket and a bucket.

Objective
To increase the children's aiming skills.

Warming up exercises
Ask the children to hop first on the right leg, and then on the left leg. Tell them to jump with both feet together. Then get them to leap with long strides.

Skill training
Ask the children to choose partners. Tell them to stand facing each other. One should be the 'mirror'. As the other child makes movements at different levels with different parts of the body, the mirror should try to copy at exactly the same time.

Do the same, but with the children standing one behind the other. Tell the child in front that he should try to 'get rid' of his partner by clever dodging.

Set up the following five stations. Divide the class into groups and get them to go round the stations in turn.

Station 1
3 large balls and 3 hoops.
The children should take turns holding a hoop high in the air. The other children should practise shooting a large ball through the hoop.

Station 2
6 large balls and 6 skittles.
Ask them to practise kicking to knock down the skittle. They should take turns retrieving the balls.

Station 3
A hoop and 4 small balls.
Get two children to bowl a hoop to each other. The other four children should try to throw a small ball through the hoop.

Station 4
3 small balls and a bench.
Working in pairs, one child should bowl a small ball underarm over the bench to the other child who lets it bounce and then bats back with the hand. Ask them to take five turns each.

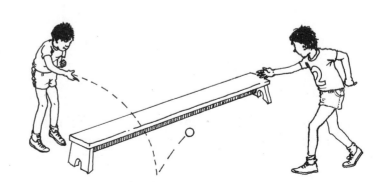

Station 5
A basket, a skittle, a bucket,
2 chairs, a hoop, 3 small balls,
3 bean bags.
Set up the equipment as shown below. Let the children take turns at each activity:

- Throw the ball into basket – underarm.
- Knock down the skittle with a ball – overarm.
- Throw the ball into the bucket – underarm.
- Throw the bean bag through the hoop – overarm.
- Throw the bean bag on to the chair – underarm.
- Throw a bean bag on to the chair – overarm.

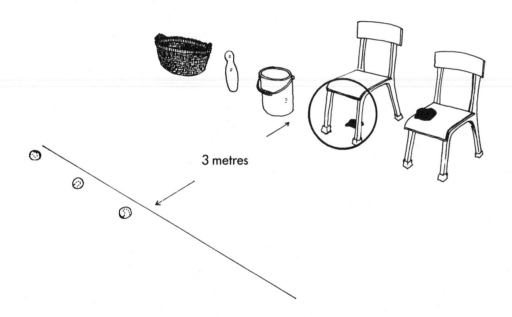

3 metres

Game
Make a circle. Let each of the station groups have a turn in the middle. Players in the circle have four balls. They have to try to hit the middle players below the knee.

Free choice!

What you need
Large balls, hoops, rugby shaped balls, small balls, skittles, junior hockey stick, bats (all shapes), baskets, junior badminton, skipping ropes, bench, racquets.

Objective
To encourage free choice of skill practice.

Warming up exercises

Soldiers and brigands
Ask half the class (the soldiers) to stand side by side in a line with their faces to the wall. The other half (the brigands) should stand side by side across the room. At the signal the brigands creep towards the soldiers. Give a signal when they are 2 metres away to 'open fire' by stamping their feet. The soldiers turn as soon as they hear the 'firing' and chase the brigands. Any one touched before reaching the brigands' starting line must join the soldiers.

Skill training
Provide the children with the equipment listed in 'What you need'. Encourage them to choose a piece of equipment to play with either alone or with one, two or three more other people. Assist the children to set up any practice they need. Then help individuals.

Game

Write four activities on a sheet of paper, for example: run on the spot, hop on one leg, balance on one foot, and jump up and down. Put one in each corner of the room.

run on the spot	hop on one leg
balance on one foot	jump up and down

Let the children skip around until you give a signal. They must then choose which corner to go to and begin the activity. You then name one of the activities. All those who have chosen that activity should sit out the next round.

Skittle ball

What you need
A large ball between 2 children,
a skittle between 4 children,
2 hoops.

Objective
To teach the game of skittle ball.

Warming up exercises
Ask the children to run anywhere. When the whistle blows they should stop still and hold their position. Repeat. Let the children run freely, when the whistle blows, they should change direction.

Skill training
Let the children practise throwing underarm and overarm to a partner. Play pig in the middle (see page 54).

Divide the children into groups of four – each with a skittle and a ball. Have them take turns to practise hitting the skittle with the ball. Repeat, but let each child have a turn at defending their skittle.

Let the children play follow my leader (see page 31). Encourage the leader to vary the direction, speed and type of foot pattern.

Working in pairs let them take turns trying to mirror the other child's actions.

Ask the children to jump on the spot with both feet together. On the command 'change' they should switch to astride jumps. Repeat.

Let the class practise walking smoothly. Encourage them to hold their body erect.

Game
Divide the class into two and give out coloured braids to make two teams (if there are not enough braids to go round, choose two colours for each team).

Set up the pitch (see below) with two skittles and two hoops. (It will help the children if the skittles and hoops are colour coded.)

Begin without any rules. Give the ball to the blues and tell them to pass only to blues and to try to knock the blue skittle down. Tell the reds to try to take possession of the ball. Build up rules as necessary!

Activities for ten to eleven year olds

Ball obstacles

What you need
15 large balls,
15 small balls,
2 long ropes, 15 coloured bands,
skittles and bats.

Objectives
To evaluate the children's skill
level and their social
and moral development.

Warming up exercises
Make two lines using ropes or chalk at each end of the
playing area. Tell the children to walk as fast as possible
from one line to another.

Get the children to hop to one line on the right foot and
hop back on the left foot. Then ask them to jump to the
line with two feet together, turn and jump back.

Ask them to crawl on their hands and feet to the line,
face downwards. They should come back face upwards.

Activities
Tell the class that you want to create an obstacle course
using their bodies as obstacles. Ask them to make eight
rows of four and use eight large balls and eight small
balls.

Player 1 dribbles the large ball with his feet around the
line of players and gives the ball to player 2. Player 1
takes player 4's place. Continue until all the children
have had a turn.

Ask the children to pat bounce the small ball with the
right hand until turning to come back, then change to the
left hand.

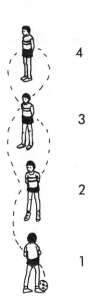

Ask the groups to make circles and pass the large ball
around. Get them to pass it underarm, then overarm.
Then ask the class to pass the small ball around the
circle. They should first pass it underarm then overarm
using the right hand. Then they should do the same with
the left hand.

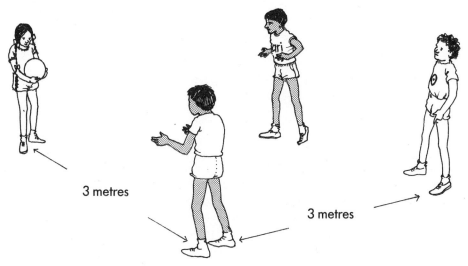

3 metres

3 metres

Ask the children to practise kicking a large ball across a distance of 5 metres. Then practise throwing a small ball underarm across 5 metres.

String a rope or put benches across the room and get the children to practise bowling and batting over it.

Give each group of four a large or a small ball and ask them to make up a game using skittles, bats or whatever they wish.

Game

Give half the class coloured bands to form two teams. Give them a ball and offer to be the referee. Blow your whistle to start. Before long they should want to suggest a few rules. If not – you will! Notice who suggests a 'new rule', who conforms, who breaks the rules etc.

60

Footwork practice

What you need
A coloured braid for each child.
A large ball between 2 children.

Objective
To improve the children's footwork.

Warming up exercises
Get the children to make groups of four. Ask three to hold hands to make a circle. One of them should put a braid into the waist of his shorts. The fourth child stands outside the circle and tries to take the braid.

Skill training
Ask the children to run as fast as possible and stop when the whistle blows (You should vary the time of running to increase their alertness). After several goes, change the rules. Now when the whistle blows, they should jump in the air.

Tell the class to stand with their legs astride and jump on the spot, when the whistle blows they should change to jumping with both feet together.

Let them experiment with different ways of running. Ask them to walk on tiptoes, on their heels, on the outsides and the insides of their feet.

Show the class how to leap from right to left foot moving forwards on a diagonal pathway. Let them practise on their own.

Games
Divide the class into threes and give each group a large ball. Play the following games:

Pig in the middle (see page 54)
Have one of the children throw the ball high between the other two who should jump for possession.

Keep the kettle boiling (see page 119)
When playing with only three children, one child must always be running.

Using groups of four children, have two bounce and pass the ball between them. The other two must try to intercept. Then play using only the feet.

Danish rounders

What you need
4 mats or hoops,
a large ball between 2.

Objective
To teach the game
of Danish rounders.

Warming up exercises
Ask the children to run quickly. On your signal they should change direction. Repeat.

Activities
Ask the children to choose a partner and stand 5 metres apart. On a signal, one of the children should run around his partner and back to his place. Then his partner should do the same.

Get the class to practise throwing and catching a large ball using a shoulder pass (first at 3 metres then at 5 metres). Next, ask them to practise underarm bowling and batting with any size ball. They can use the palm of the hand for a bat.

Still working in pairs, ask the children to roll a ball to each other and pick it up and throw it back with an overarm throw. Let them have five turns each.

Next, ask one of the two to throw the ball high over his partner's head – the partner has to move to catch it. Let them have five turns each.

Game

Use four mats or hoops for bases. They can be any distance apart depending on the skill of the players. Any size ball can be used but you should use a foam ball if the game is played indoors. The children can use the flat of their hand as a bat.

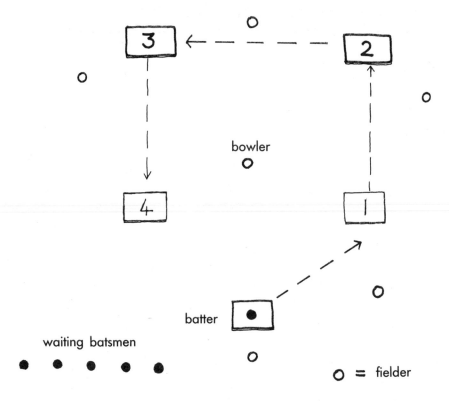

waiting batsmen

O = fielder

One fielder stands on each mat. The bowler bowls underarm to the batsman, who, after striking the ball, must run around bases 1,2,3 and 4 before the fielders have passed the ball from base 1 to 2 to 3 to 4 (without dropping the ball). If the fielders get the ball to base 4 before the batsman reaches base 4 the batsman is out. If the batsman gets there first he scores a rounder.

Let each batsman have a turn then change over. The team with the highest number of rounders wins.
NB If you have a physically handicapped child in your class do not always delegate them to the role of scorer. A child with a physical handicap can act as bowler if a chair is provided and the distance between bowler and batsman is reduced. Similarly, children with no use of their legs can sometimes move on their bottoms and join in successfully if the bowler adapts the throw and the child is only required to get to first or second base rather than to fourth base. A child with arm problems could be allowed to use the foot or head to propel the ball.

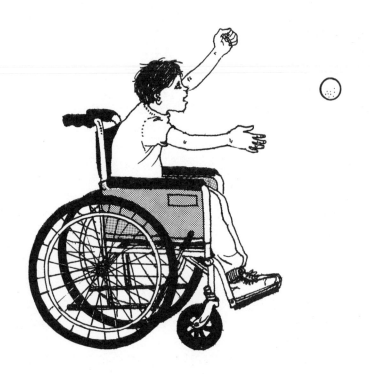

Non-stop cricket

What you need
A ball and
a bat between 2,
3 mats,
a set of indoor wickets
(or a box).

Objective
To teach the game of non-stop cricket.

Warming up exercises
On the word 'go' get the children to run across the room
and touch the floor, returning as fast as possible. Let them
rest and repeat.

Skill training
Tell the class to roll a ball anywhere in the area, chase
after it and pick it up.

Ask the class to stand together in twos. One child rolls
the ball, and the partner chases it, picks it up and throws
it back to her partner.

Get the class to practise throwing overarm, underarm
and catching. They should vary the height and distance of
the throws. Encourage them to 'make their partner move
her feet!'

Game
The children should take turns to be bowler, wicket
keeper and fielders. Let them have six balls each. The
batsman has three bats. To score a run the batsman
hits the ball then runs to the square and back. A batsman
is out if he is caught, if the bowler hits the wicket when
bowling or if he is out of his position near the wicket. Two

children can act as scorers. Choose a large foam ball
and the hand for a bat to begin with. Adjust the ball size if
necessary after playing the game for a few minutes.

Activities
Ask the children to run on the spot; gently, then quickly,
then gently, then stop! Vary the order.

Play Simon says (see page 99). Choose quiet activities.

63

Further ball skills

What you need
A large ball each,
a braid each.

Objective
To improve batting skills.

Warming up exercises
Give the children braids to
tuck into the back of their
shorts. Ask them to try to
catch as many braids
from other children as possible.

Skill training
You will need to spread these activities over three or four
sessions. Give each child a ball and tell them to throw it
high and in front, run to it, let it bounce and catch it.

Tell the class to kick the ball gently, chase after it, and
trap it with the foot. Let them practise dribbling the ball
with the feet.

Ask the children to bounce the ball diagonally away,
run ahead and catch it. Then ask them to pat bounce the
ball with right and left hand. Have the children throw the
ball up in the air, let it bounce off two extended arms, fists
clenched and together. Then ask the children to throw the
ball into the air and bat it away with a clenched fist.

Partner activities
Ask the children to practise shoulder passing. Then teach
the chest pass. Put two hands on the ball at chest height
and roll the wrists until the palms are facing the direction
of the throw. Step forward and at the same time, stretch
the elbows and snap the wrists and thumbs to push the
ball forward so that it travels directly to its target with
speed and force. Keep the elbows down before and
while the push is made. Give the children plenty of time to
practise.

Get the class to practise a 'throw-in' (some times
referred to as a 'line-out' or an 'overhead lob'). You will
need to demonstrate. Lift the ball high over the head
taking the weight on the back foot. Bend the elbows to
lower the ball behind the head and as the weight is
transferred to the front foot, push the ball upward by
straightening the arms, then swing the arms forwards.
The angle of the hands and the movement of the wrists
will alter the trajectory of the ball. Let them experiment.

With a partner get them to pass the ball and 'catch' it on any part of the body and bring it down to their feet. The partner should then pass the ball back with the feet. Ask them to experiment to find out which part of the foot is best to use to keep the ball along the ground.

Still using partners, get one of the children to bounce the ball, the other should try to gain possession.

Divide the class into groups of threes with one attacker, one receiver and one defender. Get the children to practise throwing, kicking and bouncing the ball to the non-defended side of the receiver. Have the receiver show which side she wants the ball. She will have to judge the appropriate time to move.

Have the children take turns being the referee. The other two should face each other a metre apart. When the referee throws the ball in the air, the others jump for possession. Repeat with two children standing side by side.

Games

Set up five areas and get the children to do the following:

- Practise dribbling and passing the ball, with the feet, in twos. Encourage them to move forwards as they dribble.
- Practise throwing and catching a size 4 football. They should run when not in possession, stop to catch and throw. Remind them to move forwards.
- Practise throwing and catching a rugby ball shape.

- Practise dribbling with pat bounces and using a chest pass to pass the ball (encourage forward movement).
- Practise batting a volleyball in the air as a group. Keep the ball above head height. One child may not have two successive turns.

For future lessons, when the children are familiar with the activities, you might like to make the games competitive. Divide the class into teams. For the first four activities use an end line. A point is scored each time a team crosses its own end line. They should go back to the middle line to re-start. For the fifth activity ask them to count how many 'bats' they can do before dropping the ball.

NB If these activities take place indoors it may be necessary to take each of the five areas in turn.

Cricket skills

What you need
A small ball for each player,
6 large balls, skittles, stop watch, box,
2 mats, 5 bean bags, bats.

Objective
To introduce cricket skills.

Warming up exercise

Bombardment
Divide the class into two teams and give each player a small ball. Each team throws their small balls at the larger ball in an attempt to push them over the opposing team's line. The team with the least number of large balls over their own line is the winner.

Skill training
Spread the following activities over three or four lessons:
Ask the class to face a partner across the area and sprint to change places. Let them do this ten times. Get the children to run and touch their partner's line and return. They should take turns.

Ask one of a pair to put two small balls at his feet. He should pick up one ball and run and put it down at his partner's feet then sprint back and collect the other. When he is safely back behind his own line, his partner repeats the process.

Get them to throw the ball underarm to their partner, trying to complete 20 throws before you say stop. Repeat using an overarm throw. Ask the class to sit down when they have completed 20 throws and catches.

Divide the class into groups of fours. Player 1 should roll the ball to player 2 who runs forward to pick it up and throws it back to the bowler. Have them take turns. Ask them 'Which is the best way to collect the ball?' 'Cupped hands? hands together? crouched position?'

Ask the class to practise the cricket bowling action, without the ball first. Demonstrate how to do it. Stand sideways on to the wickets (with the left shoulder facing if you are right handed) and the left arm extended at shoulder height. Look over your left shoulder. As you swing the straight right arm from the hips and begin to brush the ear, pretend to release the ball. The left hand and arm should move down 'stroking the wickets' in the process.

Move on to practising with a ball. If indoors a foam ball should be used. Have one player act as wicket keeper. It is very difficult to bowl straight at first! It is also difficult to bowl the correct length.

In the next lesson, introduce a three pace run up. Right handers will go right, left, right, wide base and bowl. Try to use a crease at this stage. Use chalk line, rope or a strip of white paper. Stress a short and regular run-up.

The children will need extra practise batting under your supervision. If you divide the class into groups you will be able to observe closely those children who are practising batting. Set up five stations with six children in each group. Get the class to rotate round each activity, giving them eight minutes at each station.

Station 1
Box or basket, small balls.
Ask the children to practise underarm throwing into a box or basket, from 5 metres, using a small ball.

Station 2
Stop watch, 5 bean bags, 2 mats.
Put the two mats 10 metres apart as shown below. Player 1 takes one bean bag and puts it on mat B and runs back. He does this five times. The time keeper records his time. Player 2 repeats the activity taking the bean bags from mat B to mat A. Then the other players take turns.

10 metres

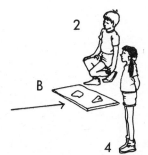

Station 3
Skittles, small ball.
The third group tries to knock down skittles from a distance of 5 metres using an overarm throw.

Station 4
Watch or clock with second hand. Ask the children to jog on the spot for a minute and then rest for a minute. Repeat eight times.

Station 5
Work with each group as they go round on their batting skills. Show them how to grip the bat and how to stand.

The left hand should be uppermost (for right handers). Both hands should grip the bat – avoid having the right index finger extend down the bat. Keep both eyes on the bowler and stand in an easy natural position. Demonstrate how to play a straight bat and show its advantage for covering the wickets.

Give the children plenty of practice without a ball first. Encourage them to lift the bat and swing forward. Gradually introduce the left foot forward action.

In future lessons re-teach the grip and stance using a straight bat then introduce a ball. To begin with you should do the bowling. Bowl gently underarm from about 3 metres. Encourage the batters to play the ball with a straight bat back to you. Then introduce the notion of pitching the ball on the 'on' and 'off' side. Place fielders and send three straight balls, three balls on the 'on' and three on the 'off'. Let the batter practise driving to the 'off', the 'on' and straight forward. Don't forget to fill in the evaluation sheet (see page 124).

Game
Non-stop cricket (see page 63) but use a cricket bat shape, a small ball, and preferably play outdoors.

Pre-athletic skills

Running activities

What you need
Whistle, stop-watch.

Objective
To improve the children's running ability.

Warming-up exercises
Teach the children that in a good running style the body should lean forward slightly, the knees should be bent and lifted more than when walking and the arms should be bent at the elbow and swing loosely from the shoulder.

Get the children to run gently and lightly, keeping the weight on the balls of the feet. They should breathe naturally and keep their eyes forward. Next, ask them to run lightly, as fast as possible and to stop on a signal. Vary it by telling them to run fast on your signal. Repeat.

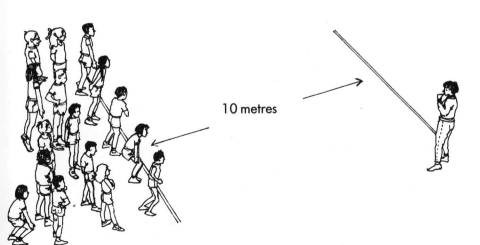

10 metres

Get the children to practise over a short distance such as 10 metres. Start by carrying out the following: 'Get ready – stand with one foot in front of the other, toes forward, arms slightly bent; 'Go!' – run as fast as possible.

Let the children do some free running, concentrating on good knee lifts. Suggest that they pat their knees, alternating the left and right as they lift them!

Ask the class: 'What happens if you run with straight legs?'
'What happens if you lean backwards?'
'What happens if you run with your arms at your sides?'
'What happens if you run without looking in the direction that you are running?'

Line the class up in teams of four, so that six or seven children run over 10 metres together. Use a starting line. Younger children find it difficult to run straight and can be helped by running to a friend. On Sports Days they could run into a parent's arms. Give older children the opportunity to time each other with a stop watch and to practise holding the finishing tape. Have many practices at starting (say 'Ready!', 'Go!') running over 10 metres, through the tape, then walking back for another turn. Older children start to 'On your marks', 'Set', 'Go'.

Games

Shuttle relay
Make teams of four, two facing two across the 10 metres. Player 1 runs to touch player 2, player 2 runs to touch player 3, player 3 runs to touch player 4. The first player 4 to cross the line raises her hand and that team is declared the winner. (You should try to spread the good runners between the teams!)

Other ideas for 10 metre races:

- Hop across on the right foot.
- Hop across on the left foot.
- Run backwards.
- Run, when the whistle blows, turn and run backwards.
- Skip across the area.
- Side-slip across the area.
- Run on two hands and two feet.

- Move like a crab backwards.*
- Give a partner a 'piggy-back' ride.*
*Not suitable for very young children.

Activities
Older children can begin to sprint over longer distances, though as a class activity it is suggested that they should not run further than 60 metres. They should also run against children who are of their own ability level.

Children should have access to a stop watch and a score sheet so that they can check their own progress. The emphasis should be on improving their own time and praise should be given for improvement rather than for winning.

At the end of term, the child who has the fastest time and the child who has improved his time more than anyone else, can be equally congratulated.

Jumping activities

What you need
Hoops.

Objectives
To develop and improve the children's ability to jump for height and length.

Warming up exercise

Jack-in-the-box
Teach the children the actions to the following jumping game:
'Jack-in-the-box' – crouch down,
'Asleep in his house' – keep quiet,
'Will he come out?' – prepare to stretch,
'Yes he will!' – jump up and stretch arms.

Skill training

Get the children to bounce on the spot on both feet then around the area on two feet. Ask them to hop on the right leg then on the left leg.

Spread hoops around the area with one for each child. Tell the children to jump in and out of the hoop with two feet together. Let them experiment. Ask them to jump backwards or to turn while jumping.

Let them run and jump over the hoop. (Younger children should run and jump into the hoop).

Let the children choose partners. They should take turns having one child hold a hoop at about 20 centimetres from the ground for the other child to jump in and out of. (Alter the height to accommodate different age groups and abilities.)

Get them to experiment by taking off with the left foot, right foot, both feet; landing on the left, on right, on both feet, etc.

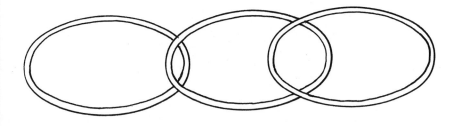

Games

Spread the hoops over the area. Ask the children to run and jump over the hoops. When you give a signal they must stand inside a hoop.

With partners, ask one child to kneel down and curl up in a low position. The other child jumps over his partner and everybody else's partner. The aim is to try to jump over everyone before you say 'stop'.

Athletic stations

What you need
Hoops, canes,
chalk, skittles,
mats, bean bags.

Objective
To improve the children's
jumping abilities.

Activities
Divide the class into five groups of six children and set up the following five stations. Get the children to rotate round the stations in their groups.

Station 1
Chalk.
Tell the children to stand with both feet together, swing the arms, bend the knees and spring forward. Use a chalk mark to see who jumps furthest.

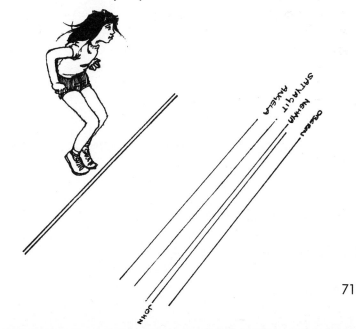

71

Station 2
5 hoops.
Get the children to jump into and out of five hoops then run back to the start.

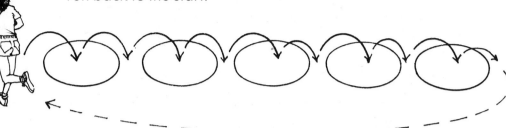

Station 3
Canes and skittles.
The children should jump over the canes, then run back to the start.

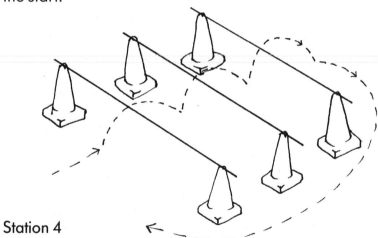

Station 4
Mats.
Tell the groups to jump over the mats (or secured pieces of paper).

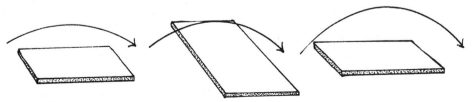

Station 5
Canes and skittles.
Get the children to jump over the canes. Let them choose their own height. Use activity skittles and make sure that the cane will fall off easily when touched.

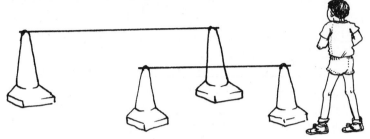

Ask the class the following questions:
'What happens if you jump with the left leg and left arm leading?'
'Can you run and jump in the air, clapping your hands whilst you are in the air?'
'Can you turn around in the air?'
'Do your arms help you to jump?'
'What do you have to do to your feet to help your jump?'

To finish get the children to practise some general throwing activities. They should have one bean bag each or one between two.

Arm strengtheners

Objective
To develop arm strength. (These activities are designed for older children only. Younger children should be encouraged to develop their arm strength through playing ball games.)

Warming up exercises
Ask the children to stand with their legs apart. Then get them to jump in the air and click their heels together before landing. Ask them to try a cross step to the side and then click the heels – ask them to try to the left and to the right.

Ask the class to make the following jumping patterns: jump forward on two feet for three, backwards for three, followed by three heel clicks. Let them make patterns of their own.

Skill training
Ask the children to perform the following skills:

- Seal slide across the area. Use the hands to pull the body along.
- Walk on two hands and one foot.
- Walk along on hands and feet with the face upwards.
- Rabbit jump from two hands to two feet.

Working in pairs, ask one child to make a bridge using both hands and both feet. The other child goes under the bridge and then visits other bridges. See who can go under the most bridges before you say 'stop'.

Get the children to play wheelbarrows – one child holds the other child's legs and walks slowly forward.

Ask the children to pretend they are caterpillars by crouching down with hands and feet on the floor. Get them to walk slowly forwards with the hands until the body is totally stretched, then bring the feet up to the hands. Let the children practise handstands.

With the weight on their hands and their feet trailing ask the children to lift their hands and clap them quickly.

Keeping the same position tell the class to walk their hands around in a circle; keep the feet still.

Give each child a bean bag and reteach the overarm throw. Get them to throw the bag for distance. Get the class to experiment with a turning throw as in discus throwing. Demonstrate the drive through the body – turning ankle, knee and thrusting from the hips as the arm swings through.

In pairs, ask the children to throw a bean bag across the room longways. If it is a nice day, take the class outside and practise throwing a bean bag for distance.

Pre-sport skills

Junior netball

The technique and general form of junior netball are as for the adult game, but some of the more complicated rules are omitted.

Before proceeding to the game of junior netball it is important that children are 'ball happy'. However, if the activities listed in the previous chapters have been followed, the children should now be ready. The official specifications are as follows:

Ball: Size 4
Maximum weight: 397g (12/14oz)
Maximum circumference: 0.64m (25in)
Posts: Height 3.05m (10ft)
Rings: Maximum diameter 380mm

DIAGRAM OF COURT

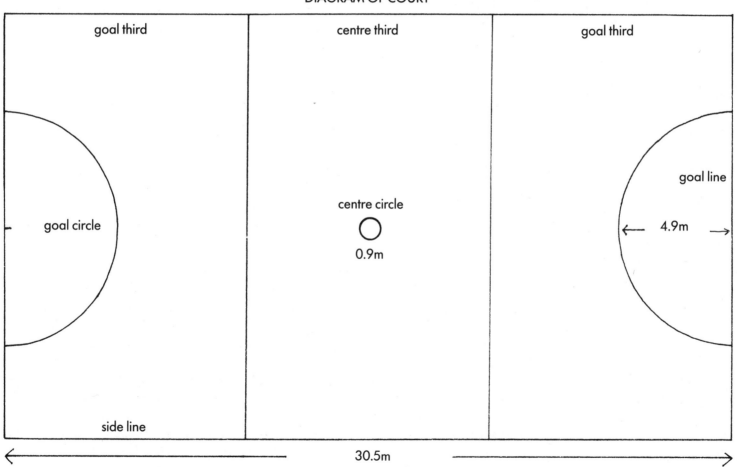

Netball skills: 1

What you need
15 large balls (size 4).

Objectives
To improve general ball skill and footwork.

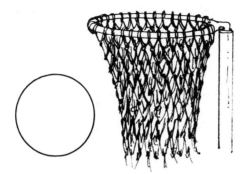

Warming up exercises
Get the class to run anywhere and stop on the whistle. Ask 'What do you have to do to stop still suddenly?' Again get the class to run anywhere but this time land on one foot when the whistle blows, then put the other foot down.

Skill training
Tell the children to throw a ball to a partner using a shoulder pass. When she has caught it, run round her and back to your starting place.

Get the class to throw the ball in the air and catch it, then throw to a partner standing 5 metres away. She catches the ball, throws it in the air, catches it and throws it back.

Tell one of the pair to hold the ball and stand still. The other child should run quickly around every standing child and back to their own partner.

Coach the children by telling them to keep their eyes on the ball and move their feet so that they can catch the ball. They should be prepared to move forwards, backwards, to the right, or left.

Netball stations

What you need
Large balls, skittles, a rope and 2 hoops.

Objective
To introduce netball skills.

Activities
Set up five groups of six children and the following stations. Get the children to rotate round the stations in their groups.

Station 1
A large ball each, 2 goal posts.
Coach the children in shooting practice using two goal posts. You will need to supervise this station closely.

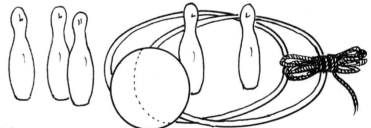

Note
When practising the shooting action, the children should concentrate on a spot just over the rim of the ring. The ball should be held high and the bottom of the ball placed on the rim. The hand should be placed under and behind the ball and the elbow pointed in the direction of the throw. The hand should be used to support if necessary. The elbow and wrists should be bent slightly, as should the knees and ankles. Extend the arm smoothly and give a final push with the fingers.

Station 2

3 skittles, 3 netballs and a rope.
Give the children target practice by trying to knock down the skittles using underarm and overarm throwing. They should take turns to field the ball and count how many times the skittle is hit.

Station 3

5 skittles about a metre apart.
Ask the children to take turns running in and out of the skittles and back. Let them count how many times the team complete the run.

Station 4

A ball between two (or three if an odd number).
Get the children to practise passing the ball across 5 metres. Each time a throw is caught successfully they should take a step away from their partner. Let them try shoulder passes, chest passes and bounce passes.

Station 5

2 hoops and 2 netballs.
Ask them to work in threes. Tell one child to hold a hoop at different heights each time and the other two to throw the ball through the hoop and catch. They should vary the passes: sometimes an underarm throw, sometimes a shoulder pass, sometimes a chest pass.

Game

All in tag (see page 117).

Court play

What you need
A coloured band each,
a ball between 2 people.

Objective
To help the players'
orientation on the court.

Warming up exercises
Tell the class to run anywhere inside the court and stop on the whistle.

Ask the children to start at the end of the court. They should first run and touch the first third line and come back to the goal line. Then run and touch the second third line and come back. Finally ask them to run and touch the other goal line and come back.

Skill training
Keep all the class in one of the shooting circles. Play catch your partner's tail (see page 17). Repeat the game with everybody in the centre third.

Line the class up on the side line and ask them to run as fast as possible to the other side line. Do the same but this time tell them that when the whistle blows they should pivot and race back to the start again. Ask 'Who managed to reach the other side line before the whistle?'

Get the children to practise throwing and catching in twos. They should run when not in possession, and stand still when they have caught the ball.

Game
Divide the class into two teams with coloured bands (eg red and green). Tie a red band on one goalpost and a green one on the other. The team with green bands on can shoot into the green post and vice versa. No rules are necessary yet. Start the game by giving one team the ball and asking them to stand on the centre spot. Blow the whistle. After a few minutes stop the game and ask if they think there should be any rules. Suggestions might be: if the ball goes off the court, the other team can throw the ball in, or, players must stand still when they are in possession of the ball.

Space marking

What you need
A braid for each player.

Objective
To help the players to
create and defend a space.

Warming up exercises
The class should face you and move on these signals:
'Run forwards', 'to the right', 'backwards', 'to the left' etc
(have them face the front all the time).

Ask the class to face a partner, and decide which one
of them is to be 'the dodger'. She should try to get away
by dodging, feinting and unexpected movements. Let
them switch places.

Play catch your partner's tail (see page 17).

SCOTTISH HANDBALL

Skill training

Scottish handball
Make the children form lines with four or five players in
each line. One player faces her line who each stand one
behind the other. At a signal the front player throws to
player 1 who catches the ball and throws it back to the
front player. Player 1 crouches down. The front player
turns to player 2 and so on. When player 4 receives the
ball she runs to the front to take the front player's place
and everybody takes one pace backwards. Keep playing
until everyone has had a turn.

Pig in the middle (see page 54)
Encourage the players to dodge from side to side before
moving suddenly to the right or the left, showing with an
arm which way they are going.

Get the class to play dodge ball in fives. One child
stands in the middle of a circle. When the player is hit
below the knee the thrower takes her place in the middle.

In threes tell the children to practise throwing and
catching the ball moving from one goal line to the other.
Coach them to spring and show with an arm where the
thrower should throw the ball.

Game
Play the same game as described on page 78, but remind
the players about the rules they have agreed on. Coach
them in spatial awareness by asking questions like
'Where is the best place to be if you want the ball?' 'How
can you get rid of your marker?' 'Reds, how can you stop
the greens getting the ball?' Ask if they would like any
new rules. Discuss their suggestions.

Netball skills: 2

What you need
8 hoops,
4 sets of
coloured bands,
2 skittles,
a ball between
2 children.

Objective
To improve all netball skills.

Warming up exercises
Get the class to run anywhere and when the whistle blows make groups of two. Repeat, making groups of three, groups of four and groups of six.

Ask the whole class to jog in the shooting circle without touching anyone.

Skill training
Get all the children to skip keeping exact time with a partner.

Ask four children to join hands around a hoop and try to force another person into the hoop.

In twos, get one child to follow the other, on the whistle the first child tries to escape, the other tries to touch her. Allow ten seconds for the first to get away.

Divide the class into four colour groups: red, yellow, green and blue.

Ask each group to make a line, one behind the other. The leader of each line takes the others in his line for a jog. The person at the back of the line then sprints to the front and is the new leader. Keep going until everyone has had two sprints.

Line the groups up side by side, on the side of the court. One person from each team takes a ball and stands on the opposite side line. Each player, in turn, runs forward to catch the ball and return it to the thrower. Coach the throwers by asking questions like: 'Where do you need to place the ball?' 'What speed should you aim for?' Coach the catchers by saying: 'Keep your eye on the ball'. 'Judge the speed of the ball so that you know the interception point'.

Get the different colour groups to do the following activities:

Red group
Practise shooting using one ball each.

Green group
With partners, one player stands near the goal post and throws the ball towards her partner who starts outside the circle, runs into the circle to catch the ball and shoots immediately. Take it in turns.

Yellow group
Standing side by side, one child faces the line at a distance of 5 metres. This child throws shoulder passes to each person in the line in turn, they catch the ball and pass it back. Change throwers and do chest passes, then bounce passes, underarm low passes, and high, lobbing passes.

Blue group
Play skittle ball (see page 57) across the centre third.

Game
Choose four shooters and give them two braids to wear crossed on the chest. These four are the only people allowed to shoot goals. Those with crossed red braids can shoot into the red goal, and those with crossed green braids into the green goal. Choose four people to stop them, two in each circle. These are the only people allowed in the shooting circles. Everyone else can go anywhere.

Revise the rules from previous games (see pages 78 and 79) so that there are no throw ins, no forward movement when in possession of the ball, only the four people allowed in each circle, and possession of the ball only allowed for three seconds.

Netball game

What you need
A netball court,
a netball.

Objective
To introduce the full game of netball.

Activities
Choose a reasonably warm day to introduce the full game. The names of players are GS=goal shooter, GA=goal attack, WA=wing attack, C=centre, WD=wing defence, GD=goal defence and GK=goal keeper.

It is a good idea to put one team into position first and talk the language of the game so that the other children begin to understand the positioning.

Make sure that the players know which way they are shooting. When all the players are in position ask them to point to their own goal. A good way to position the opposing team is to ask the players. 'Who knows where the goal shooter will stand?' etc. Once the two teams are positioned give the ball to one of the centre players and start the game. At first, concentrate on positioning. Keep the game going for five minutes and then introduce 14 new players.

It helps the younger players to understand the positioning if they are allowed to keep the same position for a few weeks. Once the players are fully orientated around the court the netball rules can gradually be introduced (see Resources page 125 for reference).

POSITIONS ON THE COURT

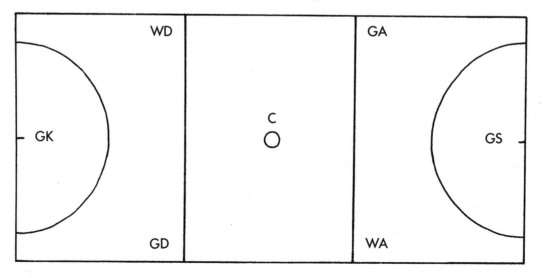

The court is divided into three. Each player has their own area that they can go in.

The goal shooter can play in area 3.
The goal keeper can play in area 1.

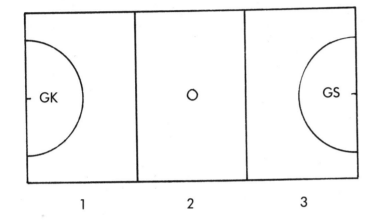

The goal attack can play in areas 2 and 3.
The goal defence can play in areas 1 and 2.

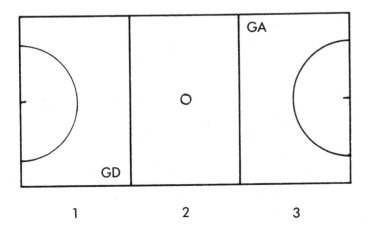

The centre can play in all areas except the shooting circles.

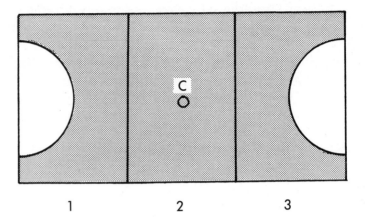

The wing attack can play in areas 2 and 3 but not in the shooting circles.

The wing defence can play in areas 1 and 2 but not in the shooting circles.

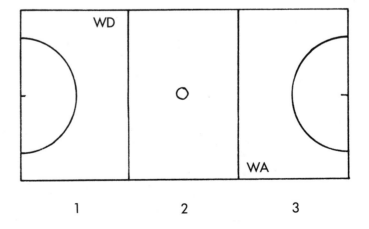

Rounders

The children should not be exposed to a full game of rounders (played to the governing body rules) until they are proficient at batting, bowling, throwing, catching, and fielding. Rounders can be played with tennis balls and bat shapes but the correct equipment can be purchased from the usual suppliers. See Resources page 125 for details of where to obtain more information.

PITCH LAYOUT

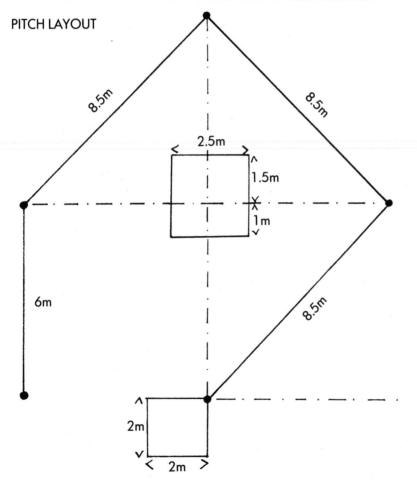

The official specifications are as follows:

Bat: Maximum length 46cm
Maximum thickness around thickest part 17cm
Ball: Maximum weight 85g Minimum weight 70g
Circumference: 17cm
Posts: Height 1.2m
Bases: Heavy

NB   Cones or activity skittles may be substituted. Broom handles placed directly into the earth are not recommended.

Throwing and catching skills

What you need
A small ball each,
coloured braids,
a hoop each, 7 ropes.

Objective
To improve the children's throwing and catching skills.

Warming up exercises
Ask the children to run anywhere and when the whistle blows, throw the ball into the air higher than stretched arm height and catch it three times in succession. Then get them to continue running.

Have the children roll the ball away into a space, when the whistle blows, chase after it and bring it back to the starting point.

Skill training

Divide the class into groups of four with a ball each. Set up the hoops as shown. Get the children to take it in turns each to try to throw the ball overarm to land in the first hoop. When everybody has had a turn, field the balls. Try hoop 2, then hoop 3, then hoop 4. If successful, move hoop 1 to beyond hoop 4.

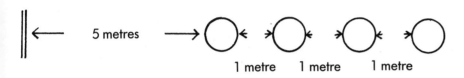

Still working in groups of four ask the children to stand in a circle to practise throwing overarm and catching the ball. Get them to stand 5 metres apart and then increase to 6 metres.

NB If there are not enough hoops – divide the class and practise these two activities together.

Game

Play team passing rounders (see page 112). Use an underarm then an overarm throw. The distance from the centre to the team should be six metres.

Batting and bowling skills

What you need

A bat (any kind) and
a ball between 2 children,
5 hoops or mats.

Objective

To improve the children's batting and bowling skills.

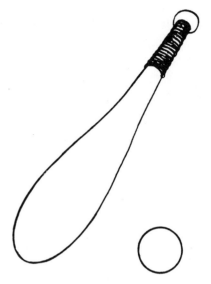

Warming up exercises

Have the children jog, on the whistle, sprint for 10 seconds then continue jogging. Repeat. Ask them to choose a spot to stand on. When the whistle blows they should sprint away from this spot. On the whistle again they should turn and sprint back to their spot.

Skill training

With a partner get the children to throw and catch a ball across 6 metres. Time them. See how many throws and catches they can do in 2 minutes.

Get each child to hold a ball in one hand. Working with a partner, have one sprint around the other and return to stand in her original place. The partner then runs around first child in the same way. Find out 'which pair can complete three turns each first'. Ask the children to practise bowling to a partner.

Coach the children with comments such as: 'Take a straight arm back; what are your fingers doing?' Get them to take a smooth swing forward stepping on to the opposite front leg to swinging arm. To encourage a good follow through ask: 'When should you release the ball?' 'Where are you aiming?' 'Where did your ball go?'

Ask the children to bowl to a partner. The partner catches the ball. The bowler then runs around the catcher back to his place.

Games
Divide the class into groups of six. Each group should have one batter, one bouncer and four fielders. The bouncer should stand at the side and slightly in front of the batter on the non-batting side. The bouncer bounces the ball in front of the batter so that the ball rebounds at waist height, level with the bat for the batter to bat. Each batter has three balls. The fielders field the balls and put them at the bouncer's feet. Keep the same bouncer but change the batters.

Ask them questions like: 'Do you think it is better to stand sideways?' 'Where should you hold your bat whilst the ball is rising?' 'When is the best time to swing the arm around and forward to hit the ball?' 'What should you do with your feet and legs?'

Play Danish rounders (see page 61).

Rounders game

What you need
A small ball each,
a bat each.

Objective
To teach the game of rounders.

Warming up exercises
Ask the class to run anywhere. On the whistle they should find a partner, hold both hands across and spin round. On the second whistle, let them run on their own again. On the next whistle they should make a circle of three and spin round.

Give each child a bat and ball. They should bat the ball up in the air, trying not to drop it. Then get them to bounce the ball downwards with the bat going as fast as they can.

Skill training
To increase the children's throwing skills, get them to throw the ball in the air and clap their hands before catching. Ask them to try to clap their hands more than once.

Ask the children to throw the ball overarm as far as they can. Get them all to throw in the same direction. They should not collect the balls until directed.

Ask the children to throw a ball to a partner over 8 metres. Encourage them to throw for speed and accuracy. Remind the players that catching a fast moving ball means that the hands must not only be cupped, but the wrists and elbows must bend to allow 'give'. They must reach out for the ball and bring it into the body.

Set up small five a side games. The distance from the front of the bowling crease to the front of the batter's area should be 6 metres. Let each batter have five turns. The bowler bowls under arm to the batter, who must run and touch 1st base and return to the batter's hoop (or mat) before the fielders have returned the ball to the bowler. If the batter is successful he scores a run. Rotate the fielding positions after each batter as follows: bowler to fielder, fielder to backstop, backstop to 1st base, 1st base to fielder, and fielder to bowler. When the batting team have had 25 balls, change over. Keep the score.

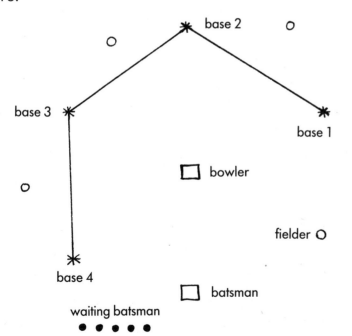

Game

- There are nine players in a team: bowler, backstop, 1st base, 2nd base, 3rd base, 4th base, 1st deep, 2nd deep and 3rd deep.
- Each game has two innings. All players must be out to end an innings.
- A good ball is a ball which passes the batsman between knee and shoulder height and within an arm and half (a bat distance) from the batsman's body. A ball declared 'low, high, wide or near' is a 'no' ball. 3 consecutive no balls = ½ rounder to the batting side.
- If the bowler bowls a good ball the batsman must try and run to 1st base whether the ball is hit by him or not.
- The batsman is out if the ball, in the hand of a fielder, touches first base before him or the ball is caught by a fielder after he has hit it.
- To score a rounder, the batsman, after hitting the ball, must run round all the bases before the fielders can touch 4th base with the ball in their hand.
- Players waiting at bases 1, 2 or 3 can choose to run to the next base when a 'no' ball is delivered.
- Players running on to bases 2, 3 and 4 can be 'run-out' if the fielder touches the base immediately ahead with the ball, before the running player reaches the base.
- The last batsman left in play, has the choice of three good balls. If a rounder is scored he has the choice of three more.
- To end an innings the bowler must bounce the ball in the batting square whilst the last batsman is running between the bases.

A good way to start is to have the following scoring:

If the batter goes all round to 4th base on one – score 3.
If the batter stops at 1,2,3 but reaches 4th base without being out – score 1.
If fielding side obstructs a batter – batter score 1.
If bowler bowls 3 no balls – batter score 1.

Association Football

The football association recommends that children of this age, learn to play the game by playing small sided games with fewer and simpler rules than the 11 aside game so as to allow greater opportunities for individual development.

General football skills

What you need
A size 4 ball
for each player,
6 skittles,
3 hoops, braids.

Objectives
To improve general ball skill
and footwork, with an
emphasis on trapping.

Warming up exercises
Get the class to make two lines. The leader of each line jogs his line forward, the person at the end of the line sprints to the leader position. They should keep jogging until everyone has had a sprint.

Play all in tag (see page 117).

Skill training
Get the class to practise dribbling a ball in an area. The ball should be kept close to the feet and the speed varied, sometimes sprint and sometimes jog. Ask, 'How can you stop the ball?'

Partner activities
Let the class choose partners. Tell the children to pass the ball to their partner across 5 metres without stopping it first. The ball should be kicked with the outside of the foot, received and controlled with the inside of the foot. Coach them by saying: 'Keep your eyes on the ball. Point your foot. Keep ready, move into the line of the ball as it comes towards you'.

Football stations

What you need
Large balls, hoops, skittles.

What to do
Set up these five stations and for the first three stations divide the children into groups of twos. Each two has a large ball. Get them to rotate round the stations. Station 4 has to be done in threes and for station 5 they will need a ball each.

Station 1
One player bounces the ball to the receiver. The receiver uses any part of her body (except hands and arms) to trap the ball. Let the ball drop and kick it back. Keep the arms wide.

Station 2
One player practises 'throwing the ball in'. The receiver traps the ball with any part of her body (except hands and arms). 'Let the ball drop and kick it back. Use the outside of the foot, bend at the knee, flick the ball.'

Station 3
Get the children to practise chipping the ball over three hoops. Then, trap the ball, let it drop and kick it back.

Station 4
In threes ask A to throw the ball to B who heads it to C so that he can catch the ball. C then kicks the ball to A. Give coaching help by saying, 'turn your forehead to receive and direct the ball, by nodding it. Use the forehead above the eyebrows.' 'C, try and judge where the ball will come and get in line to receive it.'

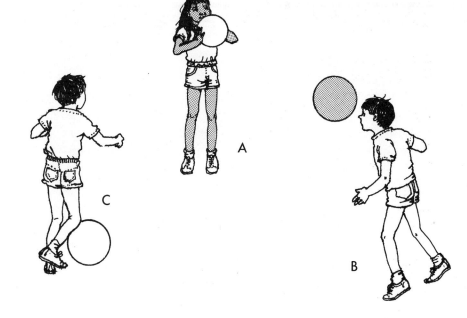

Station 5
With a ball each get the children to throw the ball in the air and let it bounce, then using any part of the body start a bouncing sequence. Get them to count how many successive bounces they make.

Games

Five a side
Set up three pitches across the area using skittles for goal posts. Start by giving one person the ball and letting her kick off on the whistle. Stop all three games frequently to talk about rules. You need to move around all three games giving coaching help: 'Keep the ball near your feet when you kick the ball.' 'Keep your non-kicking foot level with the ball.' 'Use your arms to keep your balance.'

Creating space

What you need
A size 4 ball for
every 4 players,
a braid for every
2 players,
7 skittles,
ropes or chalk.

Objective
To help players to create
and defend a space.

Warming up exercises
Ask the children to face a partner and move to the left or
right, to try to get away at speed.

Tell the class to play follow my leader in twos until the
whistle blows – then the leader has 10 seconds to put
space between herself and her partner. When the second
whistle blows they both stand still. If the chaser can touch
the leader, the chaser wins.

Skill training
In fours, one player faces the other three who stand one
behind the other. Player 2 runs forward towards player 1
showing with her hand on which side she would like to
receive the ball. Player 1 kicks the ball into the space
towards the side indicated. Player 2 collects the ball with
her feet, controls it and kicks back. Take it in turns.

Play pig in the middle (see page 54), but using the feet.
Coach them by getting the receiver to try to get free, one
to mark and one to place the ball in a space on the
non-marked side of the receiver.

Have three pairs. They will need a ball, three coloured
braids and a skittle. Draw a large circle, or use ropes to
make a circle. Place the skittle in the centre of the circle.
Three couples play outside the circle and try to gain
possession. If one player gets free she can kick the ball at
the skittle. If she hits it, she scores one point. If she misses,
the other side takes possession, but must kick to another
player before making a shot at the skittle.

Games

Five a side
Give one team a coloured braid each. Play across the
pitch as before (see page 89). Get each player with a
braid to mark an unbraided player. Ask questions such
as: 'What must you do if you want the ball?' 'Where
should you put the ball if you want to be sure the receiver
receives it?'

Ball accuracy

What you need
A size 4 ball
for each child,
15 ropes,
8 skittles
(or markers,
or boxes or hoops.)

Objective
To help to improve the players'accuracy
when playing the ball.

Warming up exercises
Tell the class to dribble the ball anywhere, practising
moving at different speeds, stopping, moving slowly,
sprinting etc.
   Then ask the children to try to juggle with the ball and
see how long they can keep it in the air using no hands!

Skill training

Ask the children to throw a ball against a wall and stop the ball from bouncing past. Then in twos, get one child to throw the ball at the wall and the other to stop the ball with her feet.

Put a rope on the ground and get the class to practise chipping the ball over the rope.

Put skittles out for goal post markers and get the children to practise scoring goals from a stationary ball a distance of 10 metres.

In threes, get the children to throw, trap and dribble the ball – A throws it over B's head to C. C dribbles past B to A's place. B tries to get possession.

Again in threes – get A to head the ball to C over B. C traps it, lets it drop and kicks it to A.

Activities

Divide the class into four groups, two will be needed for each of the activities.

Activity 1

Put four skittles at the corners of a square. Dribble the ball around the skittle then dribble it to the next until a 'dribble' has been completed at each skittle.

Activity 2

Player 1 passes her ball forward, player 4 runs on to it, controls it and shoots for goal. Player 4 collects the ball and joins the end of team A. Player 5 passes her ball forward diagonally, player 1 runs on to it, controls it and shoots. She collects it and joins the end of team B.

Games

3 five a side games

Get the groups to play across the pitch. Coach them in accuracy, 'Where was that ball supposed to go?' 'Why did you pass the ball there?' 'Who are you marking?'

Goalkeeping

What you need
A size 4 ball
between 2 players,
coloured braids,
6 skittles or markers.

Objective
To teach the art of goalkeeping.

Warming up exercises

Groups of five
One of the group throws the ball in the air and calls out another child's name. That child must catch the ball before it drops.

Tell the group to run anywhere, on a given signal jump high in the air and stretch arms high.

Ask the children to do on the spot jogging. On command: 'to the right!' 'to the left' 'high!' 'low' – the class reach in that direction.

Skill training
Tell the class to practise throwing the ball underarm for distance.

Partners
Get the children to experiment throwing by asking questions such as: 'How can you make the ball travel a long way?' 'Show me' 'Can you find another way to throw the ball?'

In twos – A throws or rolls the ball under hand to B who catches it like a goalkeeper, and then gently kicks it back from his hands to A.

Groups

Get the groups to practise throwing and catching the ball. The thrower should try to make it difficult for the receiver to catch the ball. The catcher must watch the ball and keep moving – ready to dart whichever way is necessary. The thrower should throw high looping lobs, balls to the right, to the left and low balls.

Set up 'goal mouths' using flag posts or skittles etc as markers. Put the markers at the correct distance apart (5 metres). Let the children take turns at being the goalkeeper. The strikers must field their own balls.

Game

Four a side

Have four players and a goalkeeper for each team. Make sure that everyone has a turn in goal.

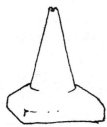

94

Coach them accuracy in scoring and in defending the goal mouth. Give individual goalkeepers information on how to cover the angles. 'Where is the best place to stand?' 'Should you be moving about?' For the strikers, 'Where is the best place to aim for if you are shooting at the goal?'

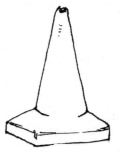

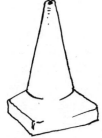

Volleyball

An adapted game for 14 players (seven a side).

What you need
7 large balls,
2 posts,
a net 2m from the ground,
any length and depth.

Objectives
- To introduce the children to an adapted game of volleyball.
- To increase their large ball skills and their social awareness.

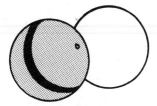

Warming up exercises

Keep the ball moving
Each team lines up at their side of the net. Player 1 throws the ball over the net for the opposing player 1 to catch. Player 1 runs round the net and joins the back of the opposing team. Opposing player 1 throws to player 2 etc, until each team is lined up on the opposite of the net that they started.

Using the same formation, call a number and these two players change places. The first to arrive in the new place wins.

Skill training
Have one ball between two children and let them take turns to volley the ball in the air. They should try and make as many consecutive hits as possible. Then with a partner get them to volley the ball, keeping it high in the air!

Ask them to try alternating volleys with a partner. How many can they do?

Have them face a partner across the net and practise overhead passing across the net. Then change to one throwing and the other volleying. After a while start with one throwing the ball across the net and then both volleying the ball as many times as they can.

Without a ball, ask the children to jump at the net and try and touch their partner's hands without touching the net. Then get them to push their partner's hands away. Take it in turns.

Game

One team member throws the ball across the net and the volleying begins. In the early stages allow volleying to take place both at one side of the net and across the net. Points are scored when the opposing team allows the ball to drop on the floor on their side of the net.

For more advanced play:
- Start with a throw.
- The ball is not in the play until one successful volley has passed over the net.
- The ball may be volleyed across the net after either one, two or three touches by a team. A player may not make two consecutive touches.
- The ball may be played with one, or both hands and any part of the body above the waist.
- A player may not touch the net.
- The ball is still in play if it touches the net.

Scoring

- Only the serving side can score.
- One point is scored each time the ball, having been in play, touches the ground on the opposite side of the net.
- One team continues to serve until it allows the ball to be grounded on its own side of the net.
- Service passes to the other team.
- A team wins when it scores 15 points with a two point advantage: 15/13, 16/14, 17/15 etc. (Local arrangemens can be made whereby a team wins when it scores 7 or 9).

Adapted volleyball can be played on any surface, both indoors and outdoors and should, after some early help, be a game which eleven year olds can play without supervision.

Five minute fillers

O'Grady (or Simon says)

Age range
All.

What to do
Give action commands prefixed by 'O'Grady says . . .' or 'Simon says . . .' Action commands not given this prefix should not be completed. The player who does complete the action is caught out! For older children, let one of them be O'Grady.

The mulberry bush

Age range
Five to seven.

What to do
Form a circle with the children holding hands and sing:

'Here we go round the mulberry bush,
the mulberry bush, the mulberry bush.
Here we go round the mulberry bush
on a cold and frosty morning.'

Younger children can walk as they sing, older ones should skip. You can vary the actions: eg 'this is the way we jog on the spot', 'turn round and round', 'cycle our bikes', 'hop on one leg', 'crouch up and down', etc.

Train stations

Age range
Five to seven.

What to do
Have four cards ready with station names of your locality. The children could make them.

 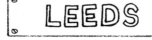

Get the children to make 'trains', holding each others waists. They can move about until you call 'stations'. The children choose a station; you turn your back and call out one of the stations. The children at that station have lost! Repeat a few times.

Sleeping lions

Age range
Five to six.

All the class lies down and tries not to move. You catch the movers.

Mouse trap

Age range
Five to seven.

What to do
Half the children join hands and make a circle facing the centre of the room. They lift their arms to make arches or 'mouse traps'. The other children can go in and out of any 'mouse trap' until you say 'snap'. All the arches are brought down. Any child still in the centre should now join the 'mouse trap' circle.

Busy bee

Age range
Six to seven.

What to do
One player stands in the middle of the room and is the busy bee. Half the class make a circle with their backs to the bee. The rest of the class find a partner by facing one of the children in the circle. You call out actions: 'Shake hands', 'Crouch down', 'Stand back to back', 'Change places with your partner', 'Stand face to face'. When the player in the middle shouts 'busy bee!' all the players on the outside change partners. Whilst this is happening the busy bee tries to find a partner. The player left without a partner is the new 'busy bee'.

Snake

Age range
Five to seven.

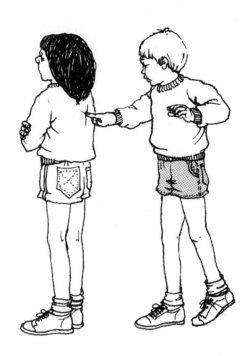

What to do
Divide the class into groups of five or six. One child turns her back to a wall. Another child draws a curly line and says. 'I draw a snake upon your back. Who will put the eye?'. Another child quickly pokes their finger on the child's back. The child is now allowed to turn round and guess who poked her back. She now gives the 'poker' a task to do. If she is wrong she has to do it herself! Change children over after several goes.

One potato, two potatoes

Age range
Five to seven.

What to do
Divide the class into groups of five — one counter and four players. The four players hold out both fists. The counter touches each fist in turn and says, 'One potato, two potatoes, three potatoes, four, five potatoes, six potatoes, seven potatoes more'. The hand touched on 'more' must be put behind that person's back. The counting is repeated until only one person is left with one hand showing. That person becomes the new counter.

Hoops

Age range
Five to six.

What to do
Spread hoops around the room (30 children — 28 hoops). Everyone moves around in the spaces around the hoops. On a command, the children find a hoop to stand in. Those without a hoop are the losers. Let everyone join in again for another turn or as many turns as you like.

Flies and fly catchers

Age range
All.

What to do
Half the class sit cross-legged on the floor. The other half move around the room flapping their wings. When the teachers says, 'Catch', all the flies must stop immediately. If a fly catcher can reach out and touch a fly that fly changes place with the fly catcher.

Letters

Age range
All.

What to do
The class stands in a line facing you. Call out letters of the alphabet. Children who have that letter in their name can take a step forward. The first person that can touch you is the winner.

103

Blanket

Age range
All.

What to do
The players stand facing each other in twos and join both hands. As they say 'Shake the blanket, shake the blanket, turn the blanket over' they shake their arms and on 'over' they turn back to back without letting go of their partner's hands.

Foot tapping

Age range
All.

What to do
Ask the children to join hands with a partner. The players should try to step on their partner's feet while preventing them from stepping on theirs.

My mother said

Age range
All.

What to do
The players find a partner and make up clapping rhymes, eg:
'My mother said', – clap both hands
'That I never should', – clap right hands
'Play with the outlaws', – clap left hands
'In the wood', – clap both hands.

Suggest they try making up other routines. Vary the speed. Let them see how fast they can do it.

Sailors

Age range
All.

Captain's coming

What to do

All players start at 'port'. The captain (you) shouts orders:

'Scrub the deck' – mime scrubbing on hands and knees.
'Clean the deck' – touch something white.
'Captain's coming' – salute.
'Sharks' – lie on stomach and lift feet up.
'Man the lifeboat' – jump off the floor.
'Climb the mainbrace' – mime climbing a rope.

When the captain calls 'starboard', everybody runs to sit with you. The last person to sit down is the loser.

'Stand-O'

Age range
Eight to eleven.

What to do
You will need two small balls. Divide the class into two groups and give each group a ball. The game starts when the player with the ball throws it high in the air and calls another player's name (from their group). That player runs to catch the ball. If she misses the catch she becomes the new ball thrower. If she catches it, the original player must try again!

A variation is for the player who catches the ball to call 'stand-o'. Everyone then stands still. The player with the ball tries to hit one of the other players. If the thrower misses she loses a 'life'. If she hits, the child 'hit' loses a life, and becomes the new thrower.

Dribble

Age range
Eight to eleven.

What to do
You will need large balls for everyone. Everyone is given a ball except five children. Those with a ball dribble it with their feet and try to keep possession. The five remaining children try to gain possession of a ball.

Fox and geese

Age range
All.

What to do
Three children line up behind each other, holding the waist of the child in front. A fourth child (the fox) faces the line and tries to catch the third person (the goose). (It helps younger children if a braid can be tucked into the waistband of the goose.)

Treasure

Age range
All.

What to do
You will need a basket of bean bags or balls. Stand with your back to the class with the basket of bean bags near your heels. The children try to creep forward to 'steal the treasure' without you knowing.

Couple tag

Age range
Seven to eleven.

What to do
Two, three, or four couples join hands and chase the free players. Anyone who is tagged should take the place of the tagger.

Ten minute fillers

Drop handkerchief

Age range
Five to seven.

What you need
Handkerchief.

What to do
The class makes a circle. One person is chosen to stay outside the circle. This person goes around the circle holding a handkerchief and everybody sings:
'I sent a letter to my love,
And on the way I dropped it,
One of you has picked it up,
And put it in your pocket.'

The one who is walking around the circle then drops the handkerchief behind a person standing in the circle. The person who has had the handkerchief dropped behind him must pick up the handkerchief and run round the circle in the opposite direction to the dropper, before the dropper can take his place in the circle. The one arriving last is the new dropper.

Hunter and his dogs

Age range
Six to eleven.

What you need
Chalk or
rope for lines,
3 coloured braids.

What to do
Choose one hunter and two dogs. The other players try to move across the area without being touched by the hunter and his dogs. Those who are touched join the hunter and become dogs. Keep playing until three are left. These three are the winners and then become the new hunter and two dogs.

Finnish hand football

Age range
Eight to eleven.

What you need
Large ball,
chalk or ropes
to divide the area.

goal line

goal line

What to do
The object of the game is to score points by propelling
the ball over the goal line at less than knee height. At the
start of the game each team waits behind its own goal
line. When the whistle blows the first six players run
forward to take possession of the ball. The ball should be
batted by hand and always stay below knee height.
Players may defend their line by blocking the ball with
their lower legs but may not kick it. On the command
'change', players on the pitch change places with those
waiting behind the goal line.

Over the legs relay

Age range
Six to eleven.

What to do
Make teams of five and have two teams sitting facing
each other with their legs sticking out in front of them.
Each person is given a number from one to five. When
you call a number those players have to stand up and run
a circle around their team, jumping the legs until they get
back to their own place. The first player to sit down is the
winner. Older players can be challenged by calling out
two numbers at once.

Skipping

Age range
Eight to eleven.

What you need
Long skipping rope.

What to do
It is fun occasionally to use a long rope and skip as a class together. Let the class take turns at running into the rope, jumping twice, and running out again. See the Resources (page 125) for further skipping games.

Birthday game

Age range
Eight to eleven.

What you need
Long skipping rope.

What to do
Each child stands one behind the other in the skipping space. Two children turn the rope and everyone chants 'All in together friends, Never mind the weather friends, When I shout your birthday, Please run out, January, February, March etc.'
NB This used to be 'All in together girls . . .'

Mississippi

Age range
Eight to eleven.

What you need
Long skipping rope.

What to do
Four children stand in line ready to run in and take the next turn. The 'winders' call out tasks:

'Hop to Mississippi,
Clap your hands to Mississippi,
Bend down to Mississippi,
Stretch high to Mississippi,
Go out to Mississippi.'

On 'go out' the next person must take the next loop or she becomes a winder. Anyone who fails to jump the rope becomes a winder.

Crumbs and crusts

Age range
Seven to nine.

What to do
Line the children in the centre of the area in two equal lines so that each child is facing a partner. One line is crumbs the other crusts. You call out either crumbs or crusts, prolonging the suspense by extending the beginning crrr... . If you call 'crusts' that line of children turns quickly and races away from their partners. If they can get to an agreed line or place before their partner 'crumb' touches them they are the winner.

City gates

Age range
Seven to eleven.

What to do
Divide the class into twos. One child stands sideways with one hand touching the wall and her arm straight. The other child begins on a given line and on the 'go' signal runs quickly towards and then under the arch made by her partner back to the starting line. Change places and repeat.

Team passing

Age range
Seven to nine.

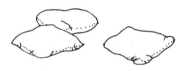

What you need
Bean bag for each team.

What to do
Keep 'teams' to no more than four. The bean bag is passed over the head from one player to another. When the last person receives it, all the others kneel flat and he side-waddles over them to the front. Each child has a turn.

Three lives

Age range
Eight to eleven.

What you need
Large ball.

What to do
All the players stand in a circle with their legs astride and the sides of their feet touching the players next to them. One person stands in the middle and bounces the ball three times. After three he allows the ball to roll. Whoever the ball touches is the first thrower. The ball is thrown at the nearest person and if it hits him below the thigh he loses a life and has to put one hand behind his back. Anyone can pick up the ball and aim it at someone else. Each time a player is touched he should put a hand behind his back. When a player is touched for the third time he has to sit out.

Tower ball

Age range
Seven to eleven.

What you need
Skittle,
a large ball.

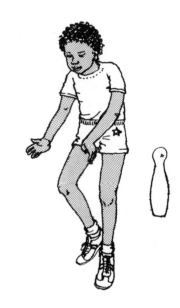

What to do
Form groups of seven or eight players. One player stands in the middle of the others and guards the skittle. The other players try to knock it down. Any kind of throw is acceptable. Whoever knocks down the skittle becomes the new defender. (The game can be made more skilful by drawing a circle of approximately 2 metre circumference.)

Dodge ball

Age range
Eight to eleven.

What you need
Large ball.

What to do
Divide the class into groups of six. One group stands together whilst another group makes a circle round them. The children in the outer circle use a large ball to try to hit the players in the middle below the knee. Time how long it takes to get the whole group out then, change places.

Wandering ball

Age range
Eight to eleven.

What you need
Bean bag or ball.

What to do
Get the children to make circles of six or eight with two players positioned in the middle. The ball is thrown across the circle from player to player, whilst the two inside try to intercept. If a centre player intercepts she changes places with the thrower.

Bounce attack

Age range
Ten to eleven.

What you need
Large ball,
skipping ropes for markers
or chalk, 4 mats,
braids of 2 colours.

What to do
Divide the class into two teams, with a goalkeeper each.
Mark two goals at each end of the playing area using
skipping ropes or chalk. The players have to try to
bounce the ball to their shooters who try to bounce it to
their goalkeeper. If the goalkeeper gains possession a
point is scored. All passes should be made by means of a
bounce and the ball may only be held for three seconds.
Dribbling with a pat bounce is permitted. When a point is
scored, the game is restarted with a throw up between
two opposing players in the centre of the court.

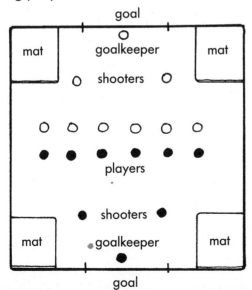

King ball

Age range
Ten to eleven.

What you need
Large ball,
skipping ropes for
markers or chalk,
braids to distinguish players.

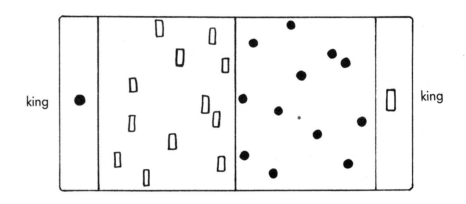

What to do
Divide the class into two teams, and let them each choose
a 'king'. The kings stand one at each end of the playing
area. The game is started with two players from
opposing teams facing each other and competing for a
ball which is thrown in the air. The team in possession
tries to throw the ball to their king. The king tries to hit the
opposition below the knee with the ball. If he is successful
the player who has been hit joins his own king at the other
end of the area. The team with the most kings at the end
of the time allowed loses.

115

Through the hoop relay

Age range
All.

What you need
12 hoops.

What to do
Line up in teams of four with two hoops laid out in front of each team 5 metres apart. One by one the players run to the first hoop, pass it over the body, and step out. They then sprint to the second hoop and slip that over the body, chase to the line and sit down facing own team. When all four players are sitting down the relay is finished.

British bulldog

Age range
All.

What to do
One child is the caller and the rest of the class stands facing her. The caller calls one person's name, eg 'Sally'. Sally runs across the area and tries to reach the other side without being caught. If she is caught she becomes the new catcher. If she is not caught all the rest of the class run across when she says, 'British bulldog'. The first one who is touched becomes the new catcher.

All in tag

Age range
All.

What you need
2 large balls,
a braid for each player.

What to do
Two children are catchers. They try to tag the others. As players are tagged they put on a coloured braid. The last two to be tagged are the new 'catchers'.

For older children you can play with large balls, which are given to the two catchers. They try to hit the other players below the knee with the ball. The players who are hit put on a braid and join the ball catchers. The last two are the new ball catchers.

Poison

Age range
All.

What to do
One person, the chaser, stands with his arms folded. The other players touch a part of him. The chaser says: 'I went to the shop and I bought a bottle of pppepsi. I went to the shop and bought some ppppeanuts. I went to the shop and bought some ppppoison!' On the word 'poison' everyone runs away and the chaser tries to tag a player. The tagged player becomes the new chaser. (If anyone moves on earlier ppp's, eg peanuts they have to be the chaser immediately). The game can be adapted to develop the children's language. Any code word can be substituted for poison eg cabbage or Frosties etc.

Restricted tag

Age range
All.

What to do
Play tag as normal, but restrict movement in some way. Some ideas are:

- Walk instead of run.
- Hop only on one leg.
- Crawl on 'all fours.'

Other variations are that the chasers may not tag with the hand or that the chasers work in pairs, holding each others hands. For older children you could make it more difficult by making the chasers stand back to back and link hands.

Keep the kettle boiling

Age range
Ten to eleven.

What you need
Ball, 2 bats,
a net or bench.

What to do
This game can be adapted for use around any kind of net, eg volleyball, tennis, table tennis, or badminton (a bench is a useful substitute).

Divide the children into two teams. They stand in lines one behind each other on facing sides of the net. Number 1 bats the ball to number 2 and then runs round to stand behind number 8. Number 2 bats the ball to number 3 and then runs around to stand behind number 9. The game proceeds in this way. Any player who fails to hit the ball back over the net sits out. Special rules can be devised, eg the ball must only bounce once before the batter hits it.

8   6   4   2

Reproducible material

Evaluation sheet for six year olds (see page 21)

	NAMES																	
Date.......................... Class..........................																		
SKILLS																		
Running and stopping																		
Hopping																		
Jumping																		
Skipping																		
Rolling																		
Kicking																		
Underarm throw																		
Aiming/basket																		
Aiming/skittle roll																		
Aiming/skittle kick																		
Catching																		
Takes turns																		
Helps to organise																		
Helps to clear up																		

Evaluation sheet for seven year olds (see page 35)

SKILLS	NAMES															
Date........................ Class........................																
Stamina																
Suppleness																
Throw underarm																
Throw distance																
Throw accuracy																
Catch/large ball																
Catch/small ball																
Kick – distance																
Kick – accuracy																
Pat bounce																
Skip with a rope																
Takes turns																
Leader																
Helpful																

This page may be photocopied for use in the classroom and should not be declared in any return in respect of any photocopying licence.

Evaluation sheet for eight to nine year olds (see page 45)

SKILLS	NAMES																	
Date........................ Class........................																		
Stamina																		
Suppleness																		
Throw underarm																		
Throw distance																		
Throw accuracy																		
Skipping with rope																		
Dribbling with feet																		
Pat bounce																		
Overarm throw																		
Catching a large ball																		
Throw underarm high																		
Catch a small ball																		
Takes turns																		
Leader																		
Helpful																		

Evaluation sheet for ten to eleven year olds (see page 67)

Date........................ Class........................ SKILLS	NAMES																
Stamina																	
Suppleness																	
Bowl underarm																	
Bowl distance																	
Bowl accuracy																	
Catch large ball																	
Catch small ball																	
Catch right hand																	
Catch left hand																	
Kick distance																	
Kick accuracy																	
Dribbles with both feet																	
Pat bounce right																	
Pat bounce left																	
Co-ordinate bat strike																	
Co-ordinate bat strike accuracy																	
Play with a partner																	
Organiser?																	
Initiative?																	
Keeps to rules?																	
Creative?																	

Resources

Books

The Development of Games Skills (2nd Edition), Andrew Cooper, Basil Blackwell

Indoor Games and Activities, Alison Parratt, Hodder & Stoughton

Mini Sport (2nd Edition), Mike Sleap, Heinemann

Netball Rules for Young Players, All England Netball Association

Rules of the Game of Rounders, National Rounders Association

The Football Association Guide to Teaching Football, Allen Wade, William Heinemann.

Skipping, Physical Education Association, 162 Kings Cross Road, London WC1 9DH

Further information

Netball
English Schools Netball Association, Miss O Place, 5 Oakdale Road, Wellsway, Keynsham, Bristol, BS18 1JQ.
All England Netball Association, Francis House, Francis Street, London, SW1T 1DE.

Rounders
National Rounders Association, Mr C Thatcher, Potters Green School, Ringwood Highway, Coventry, CV2 2GF

Football
Football Association, 16 Lancaster Gate, London W2 3LW

Volleyball
English Volleyball Association, 13 Rectory Road, West Bridgford, Nottingham NG2 6EP

Basic equipment

For a class of 30 you will need:
30 large balls – round plastic size 4,
15 rugby shaped balls – plastic,
30 small balls – tennis, foam, rubber,
30 bat shapes some preferably with short handles,
30 bean bags,
15 hoops,
30 ropes,
20 skittles or cones (stackable),
30 braids – 4 or 5 colours,

Other desirable equipment:

Shuttlecocks,
Rounders bats,
Badminton racquets (junior size),
Unihoc/shinty sticks,
Rounders balls – practice,
'Short tennis' racquets.

Games index

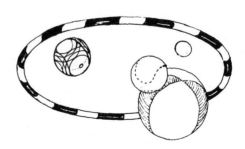

Other Scholastic books

Bright Ideas
The *Bright Ideas* books provide a wealth of resources for busy primary school teachers. There are now more than 20 titles published, providing clearly explained and illustrated ideas on topics ranging from *Writing* and *Maths Activities* to *Assemblies* and *Christmas Art and Craft*. Each book contains material which can be photocopied for use in the classroom.

Teacher Handbooks
The *Teacher Handbooks* give an overview of the latest research in primary education, and show how it can be put into practice in the classroom. Covering all the core areas of the curriculum, the *Teacher Handbooks* are indispensable to the new teacher as a source of information and useful to the experienced teacher as a quick reference guide.

Management Books
The *Management Books* are designed to help teachers to organise their time, classroom and teaching more efficiently. The books deal with topical issues, such as *Parents and Schools* and organising and planning *Project Teaching*, and are written by authors with lots of practical advice and experiences to share.

Let's Investigate
Let's Investigate is an exciting range of photocopiable maths activity books giving open-ended investigative tasks. The series will complement and extend any existing maths programme. Designed to cover the 6 to 12-year-old age range these books are ideal for small group or individual work. Each book presents progressively more difficult concepts and many of the activities can be adapted for use throughout the primary school. Detailed teacher's notes outlining the objectives of each photocopiable sheet and suggesting follow-up activities have been included.